PARENTS WHO STAY LOVERS

How to Keep the Magic Alive from Pregnancy Onward

ELAYNE KAHN, Ph.D.
& DAVID RUDNITSKY
with BARBARA WORTEN

BOB ADAMS, INC.
PUBLISHERS
Holbrook, Massachusetts

Published by Bob Adams, Inc.
260 Center Street, Holbrook, MA 02343

ISBN: 1-55850-121-5

Printed in the United States of America

A B C D E F G H I J

This publication is designed to provide accurate and authoritative information with regard to the subject matter covered. It is sold with the understanding that the publisher is not engaged in rendering legal, accounting, or other professional advice. If legal advice or other expert assistance is required, the services of a qualified professional person should be sought.

— From a *Declaration of Principles* jointly adopted by a Committee of the American Bar Association and a Committee of Publishers and Associations.

COVER PHOTO: Dale Durfee (Tony Stone Worldwide)

The names used in this book are not the actual names of the persons interviewed. These names are fictitous.

ACKNOWLEDGMENTS

Special gratitude to . . . Frank Weimann, who never swayed from his determination to see this book to fruition; to Barbara Worten, who gave of herself in pursuit of this project far beyond the call of duty; and to Brandon Toropov and others at Bob Adams who smoothed the way with great professionalism.

To Lynn Bregman and Jacob Blass, who, in their pursuit of parenthood, have shown strength, determination, compassion, and love, not only to themselves, but to their friends; to Maddy Chaber and Steve Borrowman, who pursued a dream that became reality named Charlie.

To Elaine Young, for her unswerving support and generosity, not to mention those great dinners at Nicky Blair's; to Robin Rosen, who's not only smart and savvy, but gracious and loyal, and who also throws the best Valentine's Day party in Hollywood.

To Susan Schaefer, who possesses a great sense of style, wit, and class, who enriches all she knows with her wealth of understanding, and who we hope finds office space by the time this book comes out; to Marilyn Anderson, a gifted, funny, sexy writer, who knows more about parties than Entertainment Tonight.

To Diane and Larry Lantz, whose love and concern for each other is only paralleled by what they give the people in their lives; to John and Barbara Jordan, who are not only parents, but lovers who carry on enough to be X-rated.

To Kenny Keuerman, who co-parented *Is There Life After Divorce?* without shooting his writing partner (or vice versa, we may add). To Arnie and Rachel Mann, two extraordinarily gifted writers, whose marriage proves you can mix intellect and sex.

To Beth Goodman, whose enthusiasm and strength of purpose is perfectly complemented by her personal charisma; to Donny and Debra Markowitz (and their lovely daughter Callie), whose steadfast commitment and mutual respect shows that a great partnership can indeed conquer the world—or at least Hollywood.

To Steve Klausner and Janet Fishman, whose marriage should serve as a textbook for all those who seek a perfect relationship, and whose children, Alexandra and Josh, should serve as a role model for what great kids should be; to Mark Harris, whose wonderful photographic images get as much love and attention as children.

To Rosa Salkin, who goes beyond the call of motherhood; to Judy and Jerry Pitkowsky, for always being there; to Esther and Jack Herman, Jackie Marks and Jefrey Abrams, Joan and Bernie Kaplan-Levine, Sally Rossi, Jane Weller, Anne and Marvin Sheldon, Archibald Schmuck, and Allen and Ina Rosen.

To Cathi and Brian Haehley, Rita and Steve Rosenzweig, Dominique Cherqui, Nicole Devault, Andrea and Yvette Fiano, Simone and Mario Diament, Judy and Jerry Fox, Norman and Madeline Barotz, Magda and Joel Katz, Chuck Kolb, Glen Morris, Judy and Alan Kahn, and Dorothy and Larry Brolin, each of whom contributed in a very special way.

And particular gratitude goes to Sam and Mollie Rudnitsky, who, despite the fact that they had David, continue to be lovers after 47-plus years of marriage!

❖ ◆ ❖

Dedicated to all those who so generously shared with us
the joys and sorrows of parenting.
Their openness and honesty makes it possible for others
to learn from their experiences.

TABLE OF CONTENTS

Note: Rather than chapters, the book will be divided into nine survival stages. These will provide a time-table for potential points of stress.

INTRODUCTION

Parenthood is filled with expectations of deep joys and satisfaction. Indeed, it presents an opportunity for sharing that is unequaled by any other human experience. Couples naturally expect a baby to bring them closer together, yet many find themselves unprepared to handle the stress a baby can create. Before conception, through pregnancy, until birth and beyond, the transition to parenthood presents constant challenges to a couple's relationship.

The only way to be prepared to meet these challenges is to first anticipate them, then understand them, and finally work out a mutual formula for dealing with them. When this is done, parenthood can abound with unique pleasures.

This book is not a parenting guide or a child psychology manual. It will emphasize a couple's union as husband and wife. Notice we said husband and wife, not mother and father. There's a crucial reason for this distinction. When a child enters the picture, the dynamics of a couple's living situation changes dramatically. Where once there was one relationship, suddenly there are four: husband/wife, mother/father, father/infant, mother/infant. It's these new relationships that can substantially affect the way a couple relates to each other.

But there's no reason for these changes to be negative. When husbands and wives are adequately prepared to meet the pressures they may be subjected to, they can support each other in their new roles. Through the years, books in this field have focused almost exclusively on infant care, ignoring the importance of parent care. Few couples had access to information concerning *their* personal needs and *their* development through the child-bearing years. Now we understand that being a good parent doesn't mean surrendering individual identities and interests. A strong and resilient marital bond extends beyond the roles of mother and father. And this is vital for raising children who are healthy and well adjusted.

To provide as complete a perspective as possible, this book is divided into nine survival stages, beginning with the preconception decision-making months and ending with three months after birth. Each of the nine sections details the special situations and reactions facing a couple during each period of development.

Sometimes new parents are concerned that their feelings are strange or perhaps even abnormal. For this reason, even when the relationship has been open and trusting before, many find themselves reluctant to confide in their partners. But there's no reason for these kinds of emotional barriers to exist between a couple, because the fears and insecurities that accompany parenthood are almost identical for all people.

The research for this book has been derived from case studies and comprehensive interviews. The case studies involved couples who were observed from before conception to three months after the birth of their child. The in-depth interviews were conducted on the basis of a representative sampling of couples throughout America. We asked them about the strengths they found in each other and the weaknesses; we asked them about their fears and fantasies, triumphs and setbacks. Most of all, we wanted to know exactly how they survived, what obstacles they had overcome, the secrets they had learned. Some individuals clearly wanted to unburden themselves of certain thoughts or feelings, but the majority expressed a remarkable desire to share their secrets of success with other couples who might be facing similar challenges. Ralph, a thirty-two-year-old computer programmer, expressed a strong sense of empathy with potential readers of this book:

Why am I telling you all this? Maybe because there are millions of me out there. People who are getting into this whole crazy wonderful thing wearing blinders. Let me tell you, having a baby is the most incredible thing that ever has happened to me. Of course there were hassles. But now I know how to prevent a lot of them, so I'd like to pass the info along.

We did everything in our power to collect data from as broad a social spectrum as possible, cutting across ethnic, religious, and economic lines; cutting across ages and occupations. The youngest husband and wife we spoke to were both seventeen. The oldest was a husband and wife well into their eighties, who shared with us the wisdom they had accumulated during their child-bearing years.

The occupations of our interviewees ranged from executives, office workers, teachers, students, dentists, lawyers, salespeople, artists, scientists, taxi drivers, ski instructors to full-time mothers and fathers. Approximately 10 percent of the couples we spoke to were black, and another 8 percent Hispanic or other minorities. Most of our interviews were conducted in New York and Los Angeles, but we also spoke to people from Boston, San Francisco, Kansas City, New Orleans, Houston, Chicago, Las Vegas, as well as a number of other smaller urban and rural centers.

However, we didn't want to limit ourselves exclusively to married couples. We felt that divorced or separated partners could also shed considerable light on the stress a baby can create. In relating their experiences to us, most of them had a firm agenda of do's and don'ts. Twenty-six-year-old Nancy, a student nurse, was no exception:

> *You bet I would have done something differently. I would have waited another year, maybe two or three, till I was out of school and financially on my feet. We were only married for five months when I became pregnant. That was much too fast. My advice is wait. Wait until you know you can handle the responsibility—and each other!*

Although our sample included divorced persons like Nancy, most of our respondents were couples who had positive feelings about becoming parents and who were determined to maintain a solid and loving relationship with each other. In short, we found numerous success stories, men and women who had learned how to lead emotionally satisfying lives while grappling with the pleasures and pressures of an infant.

Where did these people come from? In the beginning, we started out by asking friends and associates to provide the names of couples who met our basic criteria. When the word got out, the situation mushroomed far beyond our expectations, and we found ourselves deluged with volunteers. Many of these couples were in the process of reassessing what it meant to be husband and wife in the context of being parents. They were taking a hard and critical look at what their presumptions were (frequently based on cultural stereotypes) and how these measured up against the reality of parenthood. In many instances, we were the catalyst for them to voice these thoughts out loud. Arthur, a twenty-eight-year-old architect, spoke about his adjustment to parenthood:

> *There were times I felt jealous because they seemed so close. It usually happened during breastfeeding. But then I realized how stupid that was and I jumped right into the situation—sat down right next to my wife, put an arm around her, held the baby's hand. The trick is to get all that insecure crap out of your head. It's not them, or me, it's us, forever, always remember that. Then you can immerse yourself in all those beautiful feelings flowing back and forth.*

Since many of the subjects discussed were of an extremely personal nature, we wanted to create an atmosphere of complete security and relaxation. Therefore, from the outset, couples were assured that all identifying material would either be deleted or altered to protect their anonymity. Nonetheless, we discovered that even these measures were not sufficient to guarantee the frankness we desired. It was apparent that certain individuals had reservations about discussing particular subjects or feelings in front of their spouse. This was understandable, since we were probing attitudes and opinions they were often shielding from their partners.

We resolved this problem by conducting three distinct

types of interviews. The first was an in-depth discussion with husbands and wives together. In the second type of interview, when it seemed as though one or both persons were uncomfortable responding in the presence of their spouse, the couple was seen initially together and then separately. A third type of interview focused on those situations in which only one parent was available. These included single parents (divorced or never married), and those persons whose partner was either unwilling, unavailable, or uninvited. The type of question-and-answer sessions that offered the most intriguing insights were those in which one partner was spoken to separately after the joint interview. Marie, a housewife two months pregnant, showed us a very different side of herself in a follow-up interview:

> *I'm scared I won't be able to handle it. But it's hard to tell Steve how I feel. He wants a child more than anything else in the world. And the truth is, when you have a great guy like Steve around, you don't want to do or say anything that could send the whole marriage down the tubes.*

Naturally, in these types of subsequent interviews, we insured the confidentiality of one spouse's statements from the other.

Another issue that came up again and again were feelings of ambivalence during pregnancy. So did family pressure and the financial strain of parenthood. But the area we found to be of paramount concern to most couples was the impact a newborn had upon their private romantic lives. Through our discussions, there was no doubt that carrying a child had a profound effect on women's sexual attitudes as well as the men's. Wives were concerned that their husbands would lose interest in them as they lost their figures; and many men wondered, especially after organizing their weary existence around the baby's needs, if their sex lives would ever be erotic and spontaneous again. Taking advantage of their anonymity, many couples discussed this subject in great detail and spoke about specific sexual problems quite freely, perhaps searching for some kind of guidance or resolution. Despite occasional queries from some couples for specific comments or evaluations, we strove to maintain a nonjudgmental approach. Ultimately, our impartial stance made it possible for couples to reveal very intimate occurrences to us. Bob and Judy, both in their late twenties, disclosed how they kept sex exciting despite the fatigue caused by the baby:

> *What's the answer? Schedule your intimate moments around the baby's nap time. Put the baby in bed in another room—where he won't be disturbed by you. Ease him into the nap, let him feel warm and comfortable and loved. Take my word for it. When you have a three-month-old baby, it's the only practical way to really have good sex.*

Yet not only must a couple adjust their physical relationship to the arrival of a baby, they must also rework their connection to people outside their immediate sphere. Perhaps nowhere does this become more apparent then in the couple's relationship with their parents. Over and over, we were told how incredibly supportive and helpful grandparents had been, especially when the couples had turned to them for baby-sitting relief and crisis intervention. Nevertheless, sometimes in the same breath, we also heard how they occasionally undermined their children's confidence in themselves as parents or had somehow contributed to creating a rift between them. Diane, the thirty-year-old mother of a small infant, recalled one such incident:

Boy, the fight we had was a lulu! His parents said let the baby cry. Mine said pick it up. Let it cry. Pick it up. Finally we decided enough was enough! As much as we loved them, we eventually decided to trust our own instincts first and our parent's advice second. Believe me, that's the only way to avoid major hassles.

Another area of stress, commonly cited throughout our interviews, were the reactions of friends to the birth. Many husbands and wives confessed that even some of their closest friendships had changed after the baby was born, and often this had a disquieting effect. Infants take time, effort, and a lot of energy. Couples soon discovered that social calendars had to be drastically curtailed or eliminated to meet the needs of the newborn. Since they were often weary, especially during the months the baby was waking up periodically during the night, they couldn't maintain the same level of contact with friends as before. New responsibilities meant a reordering of social priorities. One general trend we discovered was that, during this period, many of the couples found themselves drawing closer to other people with small children and farther away from those who had none. While this social transformation is not surprising to psychologists or people who've had children, many times it catches some new parents completely unaware. One mother commented on her experiences with old friends and new:

When Andrea and I were roommates at UCLA we were

practically inseparable. I hardly even knew Susan. She was just another girl in the dorm, kind of quiet, withdrawn, you know, the shy type. Anyway, after I gave birth, it was really hard for Andrea and me to connect. I mean we tried. But I guess we just drifted apart. What's funny though, since Susan moved into my condo complex, she's become my best friend. Her baby is the same age as mine and now we do almost everything together!

When conducting the personal interviews, the questions of whether or not individuals would respond differently depending on the sex of the interviewer was also considered. To determine if this had any bearing on our study, several early interviews were conducted between participants of the same sex and then repeated with interviewers of the opposite gender. Overall, the differences were negligible. Only when it came to describing certain sexual feelings in graphic detail were males more candid and straightforward when talking to a male interviewer. On the other hand, these same men were often more open about discussing their insecurities and vulnerabilities when speaking to a female questioner. Steve, a thirty-four-year-old electrician, summed it up this way:

It's much easier letting your guard down with a woman. I know [she's] not sizing me up the way a man would. When Michelle became pregnant, God knows, I went through a lot of hell. But I couldn't tell my good buddies all the things that were churning up inside and bothering me. For them I had to play the proud papa to be. It was really hard.

The general consensus among the couples was that the interviews had been a genuine learning experience. In fact, a significant portion of husbands and wives disclosed that the process of formulating replies to our inquiries had produced a number of useful insights into their relationships. One clear example of this was Ralph. Trained to regard motherhood as a "holy state," he had put his wife on a saintly pedestal after she gave birth, and then became fearful about his diminished sexual appetite for her. During the course of our discussions, he hit upon a series of connections between his physical lack of interest and his early religious upbringing. Several weeks later, amid much excitement and gratitude, Ralph called to tell us that he was on the way to re-establishing a strong sexual rapport with his wife.

In fact, after our research was concluded, we received a number of phone calls from various husbands and wives who had participated in our study. It was quite apparent that airing their tensions and misgivings during the course of our discussions had freed them to relate on an even deeper adult level, working together even more closely to grapple with a variety of pressing problems. This confirmed our early hypothesis that a strong need exists for parents to continue to talk to each other on the level of husband and wife while incorporating their roles as mother and father into their marriage.

The following chapters present suggestions and observations culled from our interviews and case studies. As we approach the twenty-first century, the fears, pressures, and expectations that an American couple face when they decide to become parents may be greater than at any previous time in history. This makes it all the more important to dispel false notions about pregnancy, childbirth, and parenthood. Free of unrealistic expectations, couples can then be guided through and fully enjoy the most challenging and exciting period of their lives.

READY FOR A BABY?

You've finally made up your minds. The two of you are ready to start a family. You're 100 percent sure this is the right decision . . . you think. Don't worry. The decision to have (or not to have) a baby will affect you for the rest of your life, so it's perfectly understandable that you'll have doubts. Whether this decision was reached relatively easily or was a long time coming, there will always be moments of tremendous fear and ambivalence. What is parenthood really like? Can I handle a baby? Do we have enough money? Will we be good parents? Will the baby be okay? How will our lives change? Will our marriage change? Our social life?

The questions are endless and understandable. You are about to assume one of the most awesome and challenging responsibilities in life—and one of the most gratifying and exciting. Unfortunately, there's no way to know how you'll adapt to parenthood until you're actually living through it. If there are no easy answers, what's the best thing you can do? Talk to each other. Recognize and express that ambivalence as openly as you express your desire to have a child.

WHY DO YOU WANT A BABY? WHY NOW?

When you decide and why you decide to have a baby will be different for every couple. Some couples get married knowing there's a baby in their future . . . some day. Some get married just to have a baby. Others are dead set against it, and then warm to the idea. Still others assume a baby will be part of their marriage, but then decide they'd rather remain a twosome, focused on careers and adult pleasures.

Sally and Dave, a professional couple I first met while counseling Sally through a career change, were surprised by their desire to have a baby. Said Sally:

> *We were driving back from vacation. We'd just spent two great weeks on the beach. I don't know if it was the thought of going back to work . . . you know, back to the same old grind. But, we just started talking about having a baby. Dave brought it up. I found it really exciting, romantic. We were all revved up about the idea, could see the whole thing. It was perfect. Then we started to really talk about it.*

The decision to have a baby is built on the interaction of a couple and understanding why they're having a baby. There are no right or wrong reasons. It's a question of knowing and understanding that your reasons are right for you. According to Dave:

> *The really hard part was when we began discussing why we wanted a baby, because that meant letting our guard down and revealing all those things we had kept locked up inside*

our hearts—wishes, dreams, insecurities. The secrets that came out were mind-blowing! We were both afraid to say it, but finally we admitted we really wanted something of each other to hold on to. You know, just in case something happened to one of us. Just saying it made us feel closer. Afterwards we knew we were strong enough. Really ready to have a baby.

HOW CAN YOU BE SURE?

You can't. But you can communicate, and that's the key. Talk. Talk. And then talk some more. This is the time to be open and honest. Communication is the key to any good relationship and this is even more so now. Revealing your hopes and fears won't scare your partner away or damage their opinion of you. Sharing hidden wishes can bring you closer together and help you to become attuned to each others needs. And, just as importantly, frank discussions may reveal areas of future conflict and allow you to deal with them before they become problems.

Talk to your spouse about your expectations, share mutual fantasies about the baby's future, picture the three of you as a family. Through your discussions you are taking an important step toward preserving your intimate, loving relationships.

WHY DO PEOPLE HAVE CHILDREN?

Couples decide to have babies for many different reasons. Most decide to have a child because they want to create something together. Others seek a child to cancel their own mortality by extending their being on earth beyond their lifetime. Still others want a child to counter loneliness.

Perhaps they hope a child will provide them with the intimacy they don't get from their spouse or keep them company in their old age. A desire to create the family that you wished for as a child is another key motivation. People who feel this and are willing to make the sacrifices necessary to fulfill that goal can make wonderful parents. After all, no one is better equipped to do this than the adult who remembers and understands his or her own childhood.

This couple expressed three of the most common reasons for having a child: creating immortality, enriching the good life they already have, and creating a bond as a couple. Of course, there are other ways to create something together. Some couples adopt a pet. Some are active in community life or philanthropy together. Some operate a business together. It's no accident when these couples speak of their joint projects: "Oh, that's our baby."

Children are also a re-affirmation of one's own masculinity or femininity. They're the most obvious proof of virility and fertility and, for some people, the real reason we're all alive. Having children is also a measure of status, a proof of worth or accomplishment. For others it's a marvelous way to create a sense of security, to build a self-contained world that moves through life with them and is the means by which they define who they are.

Another strong motivator is societal and family pressure. Even in the 1980s when there was more variety than ever in family units, the focus still remained on the nuclear family. We live in a society where we are still expected to couple and have children. Aunts, uncles, cousins, friends, and most important, parents anxious to become grandparents, exert subtle and not-so-subtle pressures on us to have children.

Jane and Frank now have one baby and are about to

have their second child. Jane says:

Ten years ago all our friends were having babies. We'd all gone to high school together and still lived close by. Everybody was pressuring us. Oh, wouldn't it be nice if we all got pregnant together. Our kids could all be friends. Not to mention that my parents were the only parents who weren't shopping for baby gifts. We almost gave in. Luckily . . . this sounds funny . . . Frank lost his job. It got us really thinking about what was right for us.

It is essential for any couple considering whether they want a child to separate society's expectations from their own desires. Once again, honest, open discussion is the best way to discover what all of your reasons are.

HAVING A BABY FOR ALL THE RIGHT REASONS

- ❦ to create a new life together
- ❦ to experience childbirth
- ❦ to be a family
- ❦ to achieve a deeper commitment to your spouse
- ❦ to be a good parent
- ❦ to give life a deeper meaning
- ❦ to relive the joy of childhood
- ❦ because you love each other
- ❦ because you love children

SOME REASONS THAT MAY BE RIGHT FOR YOU BUT DESERVE FURTHER CONSIDERATION

- ❦ to prove you're somebody
- ❦ to prove you're an adult
- ❦ to gain power
- ❦ to boost your self-esteem and satisfy your ego
- ❦ to please your parents
- ❦ to compete with family and friends
- ❦ to save your marriage
- ❦ to create a super child
- ❦ to create the childhood you never had
- ❦ to prove your sexuality
- ❦ to produce an heir
- ❦ because it just seems like a good idea

ARE YOUR REASONS HEALTHY OR NEUROTIC?

Of course this is a hard question to answer. But you may even have asked it of yourself. Clearly, you wouldn't be thinking of having a child if you didn't feel some need. The important thing to consider is whether your needs stem from a desire to fill something missing in yourself or your relationship, or from a genuine understanding of what it means to bear and raise a baby.

If you expect a child to fill in the missing pieces, you are destined to be disappointed. Another person may be able to satisfy feelings of loneliness, but not feelings of emptiness. A child can keep you company, but it cannot and should not be expected to fulfill your emotional needs.

If you're looking for a baby to overcome the shortfalls in your marriage, you're in for an even bigger shock. The demands of a child increase the stress on a relationship. It is only in rare cases, for example, when two adults unite primarily to raise a family and do not expect any more of each other, that having a baby can actually save a marriage.

If you're not sure how to sort out your feelings, maybe the following list of questions will help:

1. Are you experiencing pressure from your parents to have grandchildren? Always remember that you cannot have a child for another person. You will be the one to bear the responsibility for the child.

2. Can you afford to have a baby? Cold and calculating as it may sound, put a price tag on your baby. Add up just what it will cost to have a child: obstetrician and hospital bills, pediatrician bills, maternity clothes, baby clothes, baby furniture and equipment, baby-sitters, baby food, a larger home, and the loss of one income or the cost of child care.

3. Does one of you want the child more than the other? As we will explain later, this can work if you set up the ground rules and reach an understanding long before you're even pregnant. But there's no doubt that this kind of situation affects even the most rock-steady relationships.

4. Have you agreed on mutual child-care roles and responsibilities? Any mutually agreeable arrange-

ment is okay these days. But remember—be honest and realistic.

5. What are your deepest fantasies for your child? What do you want your offspring to be and are you willing to accept something different? Don't have too many expectations or you'll be unnecessarily disappointed and do real harm to your child. It's perfectly healthy to imbue a child with values and guide them in a particular direction, but you should never sacrifice your child's identity for your own needs. You will misss the beauty of watching them grow and develop as their own person.

6. If you're a working woman, have you thoroughly investigated health insurance benefits and maternity leave? Traditionally women chose a career that would allow time off or flexibility for child rearing. Things have changed today, and women are choosing career paths that don't necessarily run parallel to child rearing. If you find yourself in a situation that isn't totally conducive to mothering, you may want to conduct your inquiry on company policy *soto voce*.

7. What arrangements must you make to protect your position should you decide to return to work? Ask other women co-workers about their experiences. Get the scoop on company attitudes and expectations.

8. If, for any reason, you are unable to conceive, are you willing to adopt? The answer to this question can really help to clarify the importance of a child to you and your partner. If you have any reason to

suspect that you might have a problem conceiving, gather information from your physicians and adoption agencies in your area. Speak to couples who've experienced fertility problems or are adoptive parents. Knowing the facts and recognizing your other options, such as advances in fertility treatments, helps to relieve the pressure of conception.

9. What are your reservations about having a baby? What are you most enthusiastic about? You and your spouse should sit down—separately—and list the pros and cons. Promise each other that you will not pass judgment on the lists. Then compare notes.

10. What is your theory of child rearing? Do you both agree? Rent a baby. Really, baby-sit for a friend or relative and see what happens. Child rearing is always an area of conflict for parents and also one in which there are no easy right or wrong answers. The best you can do is to read, talk and develop theories you can both feel comfortable about. Look to how you were raised and your feelings about your own childhoods for clues to what your attitudes to discipline will be.

11. Do you have a mental image of your child? How do you feel about your baby being just like you? Just like your mate? Think about each of your good and bad qualities. Your child will be a product of both and of the heredity and learning that the two of you pass on. Talk about the characteristics you hope your baby will get from each of you, and how you can enhance the best of them.

12. Do you believe having a baby can save your mar-

riage? It can if your marriage is based on raising babies. But that old cliche—it only makes a bad marriage worse—is absolutely true.

13. Have you talked about paternal participation during pregnancy and childbirth? Some men are initially squeamish about participating, so it's up to women to get them involved.

14. Does the sex of the child make a significant difference to either one of you? If it really does, plan ahead. There are books out there that can help. For the sake of your own mental health, however, try to sort out why the sex of your child is so important.

15. Are you aware of the emotional and physiological changes that occur while carrying a child? Unfortunately, you may not remain your husband's little sugar plum, and he may not continue to be your knight in shining armor throughout the nine months of gestation. You may sour and he may tarnish as physiological changes and hormones conspire with anxieties to transform you both until you don't even recognize yourselves. But, take heart, it lasts only nine months—and a few months of adjustment afterwards.

16. Are you prepared to assume the responsibilities of a dependent for at least the next twenty years? Think hard about this one. Some parents say the responsibilities never end.

HOW TO DEAL WITH FAMILY PRESSURES

Parents, grandparents, and friends will tell you that

children are wonderful bundles of joy. Many parents can't wait for their newly married children to make them grandparents; some outright hound their kids. But of course, they are looking to satisfy their needs and not yours. Yet, as overanxious as some families are to see grandchildren come along, there are those who are equally negative toward having children. Remember, every piece of advice you will ever receive about whether or not to have a child—even advice from professionals—comes from their own experience and understanding. If your parents had a difficult time raising you, if having children put too much stress on their relationship, they may discourage you when you ask their advice.

DEFUSING THE PRESSURE

What can you do? If you have a good relationship with your own parents and grandparents, the reassurance of having an extended family willing to contribute to child care can make the decision to have a child easier. Be direct. Come right out and ask your parents whether or not they are willing to contribute to child rearing: Will they baby-sit on a regular basis, help with the expenses, etc. If they're not willing (or able) to help, you have every right to ask them why they're pressuring you to have a baby. Remind them that you and your spouse will have all the responsibility.

EXPECTATIONS. WHAT'S REALISTIC? WHAT'S NOT?

"We're not as close as we used to be. We're having problems. A baby might save our marriage."

Forget that. A baby can enrich a good marriage, make it even better. A baby will, however, only make a bad marriage worse. If you're expecting a baby to transform your spouse into someone he or she never was before, you can forget that idea, too.

"A baby will make my spouse love me more."

Joan, a woman in her mid-twenties, was troubled by the lack of emotional intimacy between her and her husband, Richard. Joan believed that having a baby would bring them closer together. Richard would find a new appreciation for her as the mother of his child and become less self-centered.

The sad truth is that Richard did indeed appreciate the child, but he never developed any warmer feelings toward Joan. He revered the baby as an extension of himself, and saw Joan as just the breeder and caretaker. He became no more generous with his time or emotions, and Joan's disappointment was profound.

Unrealistic expectations only set you and your spouse up for disappointment in each other and your baby. Our culture has created the illusion that fairy-tale happiness is achievable and that a perfect family world can be created. Well, no one can live up to that expectation and if you believe your marriage should, you'll probably destroy your relationship before it can begin to thrive.

MORE UNREALISTIC EXPECTATIONS

❧ Our baby will be perfect.

❧ We will both be perfect parents.

❧ We will set aside all our old differences.

Parents Who Stay Lovers

- We will be a better couple.
- We never fight and the baby won't change that.
- Our relationship won't change.
- The adjustment to parenting will be easy.
- We won't have the problems our friends had.
- We can handle things on our own.
- We'll set the rules, not the baby.
- Hired help solves all your problems.
- There's nothing to be afraid of.
- We'll never resent our baby.
- We'll never fight about money.
- We'll never be like our parents.

WHAT ABOUT ME? WHAT ABOUT US?

Parenting does not mean giving up your individual identity. And, the last thing it means is abandoning your life as a couple. Well-adjusted, happy children come from and thrive in homes where there is a strong marital bond. But, don't kid yourself. Your lifestyle is in for a major overhaul. Children at every age force you to put your own needs on hold, demand love and understanding, and invade your privacy.

Say good-bye to that socially active lifestyle and your spontaneous lovemaking. Get ready to restructure your life around an infant's diapers, feedings, and naptimes; a toddler's early morning bedroom surprises; a preschooler's rigorous social schedule. And don't expect it to get any easier as your child grows up.

Every couple expects their baby to bring them closer together. The truth is, in the beginning, a baby can actually pull you apart. During the first few months of your baby's life, you'll be lucky to get one decent night's sleep per week. You are going to be so exhausted that even the littlest problem could ignite a major blow-up between the two of you.

Six months after the actual event, the couple who shared this story with me could laugh about it. At the time it happened, however, it didn't seem funny.

Pat and I were headed out for our first real grown-up party in months. She was all dressed up, new dress, sexy makeup. She had Kevin on the changing table. Our lovely baby boy decided to do his best impersonation of a fountain. She screamed at me. I screamed at her. We never made it to the party.

THIS IS WHAT I WANT

Before you set out to have a baby, you must both reach a very clear agreement as to what you want for yourselves as a couple, what you need as individuals, and how you will try to accommodate this after the baby arrives.

Just because you may both desire a child doesn't necessarily guarantee you will both make the same adjustments to this new little person. It also doesn't mean that you will both be the same kind of parents or want the same kind of relationship with your child. In some cases, the differences are even greater. One of you may want a child and the other may not. This is a fairly common occurrence in second marriages. One spouse may already have children and have no interest in having any more. Nan and Steve faced exactly this problem.

Steve was fifteen years older than Nan. He'd been married once before and had three grown children. He didn't want to share his new wife with a demanding infant. He wanted a carefree, sophisticated adult relationship. Nan was dying to have a baby, and unless they could reach some agreement, she was going to end their relationship. She was honest enough to admit that her frustration and anger at Steve's denying her a child would create a permanent barrier between them.

This was extremely painful for both of them. Luckily, they were wealthy enough to have some very attractive options available to them.

Steve agreed to have a baby. But the baby would be my responsibility. I'd stay home. That would be the time I spent with my child. He expected to have me all to himself in the evening. So, I had to structure my day so the baby was all taken care of—in bed, fed—before he came home.

Raising a child with one nonparticipating parent may not be an acceptable solution for everyone. Nan, however, found it worked for her and was preferable to ending her relationship with the man she loved. The important lesson here is that the standard traditional family experience may not be what works best for you. Healthy children and happy marriages are the result of individual family units meeting the needs of all the family members in their own unique way.

Now, if one person is giving in to another's wishes under duress, or is simply humoring them because they expect a change after the baby, watch out. The husband who enjoys traveling as a photojournalist isn't going to suddenly get a job as a shoe salesmen so he can stay home. The wife who's finally made it as an actress, isn't going to just pack it all in. If you want your relationship to be an honest and loving one, you must agree to willingly accept and accommodate each other's needs long before the baby is born.

In deciding to have a child, you must both look very closely at your relationship and assess its strengths and weaknesses, what you each find rewarding and what you'd like to change. Sometimes people are not aware of their real needs, their faults, or their assets. This dialogue will help you to develop an honest vision of each other as parents. It will also help you to develop enough confidence to accept your individual style of parenting and save you from struggling to conform to some super-Mom or super-Dad image created by media hype or competition with friends. Throughout these discussions keep in mind that you can be honest without being brutal. We are all more likely to accept suggestions posed in a positive way than those that seem critical or judgmental. Be kind with your partner. Part of having a good relationship is being able to accept the other person's self-image. Don't ever tell the person you love that they're simply not who they think they are. This isn't going to endear you to them, and it could start a very destructive confrontation.

I knew that Aileen wouldn't be happy staying at home with the baby for long, but she insisted. I couldn't tell her that it wasn't going to last. Who was I to pass judgment. And, if I said she was wrong . . . well, she'd really dig her heels in and we'd be nowhere. Instead, I suggested that she take a leave from work rather than just quit—keep her options open. I pushed this idea along by reminding her that we would really benefit from her continued medical coverage!

At this point, neither of you know what you'll be like as parents, nor can you envision absolutely what your partner will be like. What's important here is to be honest about the qualities you see in each other while remaining supportive and caring. At least you should be able to relieve each other from the stress of adapting to someone else's idea of the perfect parent.

WHAT ABOUT A TEST DRIVE?

If you want to take a trial-run at parenting, spend the weekend with friends who have children. Volunteer to baby-sit for a weekend or take a friend's child for a trip to the beach. While this will never be a totally accurate representation of the future with your child, it can be a helpful exercise.

Observe your friends and their children, and formulate your own opinions of how children are affecting their lives. What do the biggest problems seem to be, and what might you do in that situation? Ask your friends about their experiences, but remember the answer you get will depend on the experience of the moment. If your friend has just had an argument with her two-year-old, you may not get the most positive response. Ten minutes later, after the child hugs her, however, she may bore you silly telling you how children are the most wonderful experience in the world.

Like any of life's major events, parenting is a learning and growing experience. If you approach it with the right attitude you will become more comfortable with it and more secure in your knowledge of what's right and wrong for you.

SPARE THE ROD? SPOIL THE CHILD?

Everyone has their own definition of what a good parent is. To be a successful mom-and-dad team you don't need to have the same theory of child-rearing, but it helps to know what you're planning before the blessed event.

Conflicting attitudes toward discipline, for example, can result in some very tense moments for a couple. A couple who can't accept each others' differing beliefs are out for a very rocky ride. The arguments that spring from this sort of disagreement are the worst parenthood has to offer. Fighting over the kids, particularly in front of them, can destroy a marriage and a child.

Children need balance. Right from the beginning you must accept each other's rules, even if they are different rules. Give your partner enough room, allow him or her to treat the child the way he or she thinks best. This can be hard, but it is necessary to preserve a healthy home. If you find you do have irreconcilable differences in your attitudes toward spanking, the use of alcohol and drugs (including smoking), and religion, find noncombative ways to discuss your differences. This is the time to consult a professional. A therapist can provide the objective counsel necessary to get beyond the immediate impasse to the real source of your problems. A professional can also help you to reach agreements and keep both of you honest in holding to those agreements.

And, children must understand the rules, but differing attitudes and expectations from each parent are not necessarily bad for your child. Children quickly learn that parents may have different standards and expectations. If given the freedom, children also learn how to get the best from each parent. As long as you and your spouse honestly accept each other's differences, there really should be no long-term negative effect on any of you.

LISTEN TO EACH OTHER

If your partner says, I know I will not be this type of a parent and tells you so over and over again, then you must listen and believe what that person is saying. After the child is born that person is not going to change, and a spouse who believes otherwise is in for a tremendous disappointment. On the other hand, when a couple is motivated, and their heart is in the right place, they can become even more than they expected and see beyond all their anticipated problems.

Even before we were married, Hank and I would talk about the children we would have—even gave them names. We didn't really know what to expect, but we knew it would be wonderful. And you know what? It was. We were so over-joyed at our great achievement that we could sit for hours marveling at the perfection of baby Samantha's toes. We cherished each other more for having done this together— just like I knew we would!

The truth is that many new parents are so over-whelmed by the miracle of life that they do undergo a somewhat miraculous transformation of their own.

You can never really predict what someone will be like when they're confronted with reality. I knew I'd be OK but I was really worried about Jack. He was used to a lot of freedom— hanging out with his buddies. He kept telling me not to worry, but he was so careless and irresponsible. I didn't think I'd ever be able to leave him alone with the baby. Well, surprise, surprise. People really can change. From the day I came home with Michael, Jack has been the most devoted and patient father I've ever seen. Now he watches the ballgames with the baby.

THE REWARDS

❦ Our lives were so enriched by our baby.

❦ Our love for each other was renewed, maybe even intensified.

❦ We both felt we finally found a deeper meaning to life.

❦ All the little annoyances on the job seemed to be meaningless; the baby, the family was suddenly the most important thing in the world.

❦ The depth of the selfish love you feel for your baby is staggering.

❦ We couldn't take our eyes off the baby; it really was a miracle.

❦ We experienced moments that I could only describe as intense bliss.

❦ We learned so much about ourselves.

❦ The joy at looking at this little life we'd both created is greater than anything we'd ever known.

HIRED HELP

Everybody who is planning a baby has some expectation that hiring baby-sitters, enlisting the aid of relatives, or hiring a full-time housekeeper will enable them to have some time off. First of all, unlike parents, a housekeeper gets two days off, so even with hired help there are still demands. You may also discover that you have an inbred fear your hired help will never care for the baby the same way you would. This is particularly true in the first six months. There is no hired help in the world as reliable as a loving parent.

Then comes the important question, if you're not planning on spending any time with your baby, why are you bothering to have it? Of course, jet setters and movie stars have children and don't seem to worry much about how they're going to care for their children. The trick for the rest of us is finding a way to live a normal life and still give your child enough attention.

In the last twenty years we have given a lot of credibility to quality time over quantity time. This is a nice trendy phrase that may be nothing more than an easy way for working mothers to rationalize their return to work. Ultimately, the merits of this can only be determined by each individual. If the stress of leaving your baby with a sitter is so great that you can't concentrate at the office and suffer tremendous guilt, you should be searching for a different arrangement. As parents you have to do what keeps you both sane and produces a healthy, happy child, couple, and home life.

Interestingly, we are currently witnessing a return to the one-parent-at-home-one-parent-at-work family. In some cases Dad is the one at home. But, mostly Mom is assuming the role of principal caretaker. Why is this happening? Well not all women have gratifying jobs that they are anxious to keep. Other women have, to their own surprise, discovered the satisfaction of child rearing; others work at home. Being a mother and homemaker no longer seems to carry the same negative cache as housewife. Some child-care experts contend that the reason for this phenomena is simple— traditional childrearing simply works better.

WHEN DID I BECOME MY MOTHER? WHEN DID I BECOME MY FATHER?

The time to decide how you will take care of your baby—what will be Daddy's responsibilities, what will be Mommy's responsibilities, what you will share—is long before your baby is born. Child-care responsibilities should be a big part of your decision to have or not to have a baby. If you long to remain a loving couple, it's important that you both honestly express what you need as individuals: who will work full-time, who won't, who's going to be getting up in the middle of the night, and so on.

Since the only role models some couples have to draw on are their own parents, under stress they may find themselves following personally damaging patterns that they swore they'd never repeat.

Women, by nature, are more physically attuned to their baby's needs. Sometimes, particularly if the woman is breastfeeding, the man can feel left out, and actually withdraw from his wife and child. If left unchecked, the husband in this situation becomes an uninvolved outsider, and the wife gradually assumes more and more responsibility. This is certainly not going to keep any romance alive.

I was working with a bright professional couple. They had a three-month-old boy and were both holding down full-time jobs. Since the birth of their baby, Edie, the wife, was riding her husband, Bob, a lot. They were bickering and saying things to each other they would never have imagined voicing before.

EDIE: When the alarm would go off at 6:30 every morning, I would lie there like a zombie. Bob would be up and at 'em. He'd slept through the night. I'd been up at least three times.

I hated him. In the afternoon, when I'd be falling asleep in my office, I'd hate him even more.

BOB: Edie was a total monster. And I didn't see how it was my fault. Before the baby, we'd decided to share the nighttime feedings. She was the one who took it upon herself to get up and do it all.

Once they were able to start talking, Edie realized that Bob had never dumped the responsibility on her. She had just assumed it on her own. Once they got back on track with their original plan of shared responsibility, their feelings about each other improved. This example reinforces two points. Planning is important, and talking things through must continue throughout every phase of your child's life. Nobody loves a martyr or a loafer. If you're not happy about your partner's behavior, talk. Even it it's a difficult subject to broach and tempers get a bit hot, it's better to air your feelings than to let them eat away at the love you feel for each other.

IS THIS THE RIGHT TIME TO HAVE A BABY?

Are you in a state of mental readiness to have a child? Do you have realistic expectations of what a child is going to do for the two of you? Have you recognized the things a baby can't do for you? Are you ready and willing to sacrifice your own needs? Are you strong enough as a couple and as individuals to ride out the upheavals?

Linda and Alan have been married for ten years and are about to have their first child. In the early days of their marriage they were confronted with the possibility that Linda was pregnant. While they were both excited about the prospect of having created a life together and knew that at some point they wanted children, they both felt this was not the right time to start a family. Luckily, Linda was not pregnant.

Now, nine years later, both Linda and Alan are comfortable in their marriage. They are a strong twosome with a clear idea of who they are as individuals. They accept themselves and they accept each other. They have also been able to put the responsibilities of having a child into healthy, realistic perspective.

Linda, the oldest of five children, has recognized that having her own baby will be very different from her teenage baby-sitting. Bruce, an only child, is no longer troubled by the thought of sharing his wife with someone else. They are now so connected as a couple that the thought of having a child is a natural evolution. The level of trust and openness they share is so deep that it will support them through all the fears and difficulties they will face. This connection, the trust and openness, are all important indicators that you are ready to be a parent. That doesn't, however, negate the fact that you may still be terrified.

UNPLANNED BUT WANTED

Even though an unplanned baby may be a tremendous shock and disrupt the early romantic years of your marriage, it can and does work out for many couples.

If the wedding had not been planned so far in advance, nobody would have believed us, but yes, Carrie got pregnant on our honeymoon. I guess all the excitement threw her hormones out of whack or we miscalculated. This baby was certainly unplanned, but wanted, so with the help of Carrie's parents, we rearranged our schedules and our lives. Things have worked out better than we could have imagined. We actually finished all our schooling and raised two kids at the same time!

MONEY MAKES THE WORLD GO AROUND

One thing that is really terrifying about having a child today is money. Children carry a high price tag. The latest estimate is that is costs approximately $100,000 to raise a child to age eighteen. Most families dependent on two incomes have to carefully assess how they will make the adjustment.

DO YOUR ARITHMETIC

Add up just how much it will cost to have a baby. Here's a list of what your first year expenses are likely to entail.

- obstetrician and hospital bills
- pediatrician bills
- maternity clothes
- baby clothes
- baby furniture and equipment
- baby-sitters
- baby food
- a bigger house
- the loss of one income

Then do a basic budget: housing costs, insurance, taxes, utilities, food, transportation, entertainment, and the treats you both need. Evaluate where your money comes from and how you have handled it in the past. Look at who earns what and how that affects your position in the family. Spend a week or two writing down every expenditure. This activity will give you a clear idea of where your disposable income goes

Now, you may not find comfort in your financial status, but early warnings help you to plan ahead and find solutions.

As the cost of living the good life rises, some men may be terrified by the prospect of being the sole wage earner, not only responsible for two adults, but also a helpless child. Some women panic at the thought of being totally dependent. These are feelings that need to be resolved before you take the big leap. Any issue can be valid or serve as an excuse for postponing having a child: wait until I get a new job, make more money, save for a house, finish the sailing season. Now, sometimes couples postpone having a child in the name of financial security when what they should be looking at is whether they truly want a child at all.

> *One day it struck me that Zack and I were approaching our 40th birthdays. Even though we always said that we didn't want to be old parents, we had never said we really wanted a baby or found the opportune moment to have one. I don't know if we really do want a baby, but I know we have to discuss it soon or Zack won't be having a baby with me.*

SHARING YOUR DECISION
Now that you've worked out all the kinks and really

feel comfortable with your decision to have a baby, do you keep it a secret or tell the people closest to you?

This is a very personal decision. Some people are anxious to keep their plans private, while others want to share them with family and friends. Although this is not always true, women generally want to talk, while their husbands want to keep this news to themselves. Women often seek counsel from their friends and are anxious to get medical advice and opinions. Whatever your decision, you must both accept and respect it.

If you do decide to tell people, don't be shocked if you get widely differing responses. Many people will be wildly enthusiastic. Some people, however, will tell you quite openly that they think you're mistaken. You might hear this from single friends who know a baby will change your relationship and who want to keep things between you as they are. Remember, no matter what response you get, it has nothing to do with your decision and everything to do with the other person's feelings or conflicts about children.

IN CONCLUSION

For all the negative things you can imagine happening when you bring your baby home from the hospital, there are many, many more positive ones. You've created something beautiful together. You will share moments that will bring you closer and touch you deeper than you could ever imagine. As you approach this next stage in your relationship, keep in mind that being a couple is your first priority. You are, in fact, having a child to enhance your union as a couple.

We can't reinforce enough how important it is to understand each other's reasons for wanting a child. Those reasons should always be a part of what enhances your relationship. Be mindful of the fact that you can't be sure how you are going to react when this new little person enters your life. Sometimes one or both new parents becomes so infatuated with the baby that they abandon their marriage for this new relationship. This is, of course, losing sight of the structure in which you decided to have a baby in the first place.

Once you both decide that you are ready for a baby, go ahead and enjoy every single moment of it. Facts are only part of your decision to have a child. The emotional yearning is important too and may even fly in the face of logic. Again, do what feels best for the both of you. Have fun with your decision and keep a healthy balance between reality and fantasy.

GETTING PREGNANT

You spend your whole adult life trying not to get pregnant, actually terrified that you will. You fuss with birth control, worrying when your period is late. Then one day you decide you want a baby and everything changes.

GOOD-BYE BIRTH CONTROL. HELLO . . . ?

Total inhibition? Total freedom? The lovemaking that fantasies are made of: Unfortunately, it doesn't always work out that way. Even if you've had the most satisfying sexual relationship up until this moment, your first sexual adventure without birth control may not be particularly earth shattering. You're taking a big step forward, making a huge change.

There are two factors at work here. First of all, sex with birth control may be a little fussy, but it also comes with no strings attached. There's little or no likelihood it will result in a twenty-year responsibility. Even if your minds are set on a baby, you are still likely to suffer from at least a minimum of ambivalence, and those feelings can inhibit your performance and pleasure.

The second factor is time. If a couple has decided to dispense with birth control and let nature take its course on its own time, they may very well be looking forward to the time of their lives. Even, in fact, hoping that they don't get pregnant too quickly. Unfortunately, in the 1980s most couples view children as only one aspect of a larger social and vocational schedule and don't feel they can afford the luxury of nature. Many couples today approach the discontinuation of birth control with the same goal-directed fervor they bring to the office. Maybe it's a carryover from their achievement-oriented lifestyle, but amazingly most men are able to function under the gun and many often perform better than they usually do. Nevertheless, many couples, even the most emotionally connected, feel some performance anxiety. Making love for a purpose, and by the calendar or the thermometer, instead of spontaneously and for their mutual pleasure, really changes their sexual interaction.

PERFORMANCE ANXIETY

Susan and Bob were both very excited and involved in planning their first attempt at conception.

Bob was so cute. He brought home champagne and flowers. I had candles burning all over the place. This was going to be a great night for us. Yeah, in our dreams. It was torture. We couldn't relax—and feel comfortable with each other, much less feel aroused by each other. We both worried sick over it.

The pressure to perform under these circumstances is

extraordinary and very likely to distress even the most sexually compatible couples. Add to this the unconscious awareness that this one act can change your whole life, and it's easy to understand why your attempts at conception can be very difficult.

If you really find yourselves fumbling around, relax, just hold each other, take a moment (or an hour if you need it) to reinforce your intimacy. Remember how much you love each other. There really is no reason to doubt your partner's commitment to having a child or their skills as a lover. With time you will become comfortable and return to your usual satisfactory sexual interaction.

If, however, sexual difficulties continue and are marked by the avoidance of intercourse or a failure to ejaculate, this could be the moment of truth—when you and your partner face your real feelings about having a baby and about each other.

MARIA: We were both hiding from each other. We knew it. We had hardly had any sex for three years. I guess we shouldn't have been too surprised that we really didn't know how to go about having an active sex life.

Wanting a baby didn't solve our problem. We ended up in sex therapy and discovered an intimacy and honesty that we had never known before.

I knew that I wanted a baby and that I loved Tony. What I didn't know was how afraid I was of giving up control over a baby growing inside of me. The thought of childbirth terrified me. I got kind of spooked, even started thinking I must have had a past life in which I died in childbirth.

TONY: I knew that Maria wanted a child. I also knew that she loved me and I loved her. What I didn't know was how an impending pregnancy and parenthood would affect our relationship. I had seen my mother use us children to manipulate my father. I really thought that Maria might do the same.

MARIA AND TONY: In the beginning we had to force ourselves to interact sensually. The prescription was just kissing, hugging, then sex three times a week. It was weird, but after a while we really got to enjoy it. We almost forgot we were trying to get pregnant. We just loved being together.

KEEP THE ROMANCE ALIVE

Though you now have a motive for sex beyond the pleasure principal, it's important to keep things in perspective.

Sex can now be even more spontaneous and exciting. You really can reach a happy medium between purpose and pleasure. You both love each other. That love has always been an important part of your sex life. If you retain that loving feeling, it will make your new awkwardness much easier. Have sex throughout the month, and don't even expect to conceive for the first six months. And, if you're really struggling for inspiration, flip through a few of those women's magazines you seem to only have time for when you're waiting for the doctor or dentist. Lots of married couples have survived this same experience. You may find some stimulating and solid advice.

Plan a vacation, a little get away, during the time of the month you are most likely to conceive. Treat yourself to sexy lingerie, and buy something fun for your husband, too. Wine, flowers, silk briefs. There is a tremendous number of sexual aids available today—books, articles, tapes, even board games. Make it your business as a couple to explore these together. And most important, remember, this is not agony, not just for the purpose of conception. This is your golden opportunity to finally enjoy sex without birth control.

TIMING IS EVERYTHING

Funny, but once you actually try to get pregnant, it's tougher than you think. You'll have to calculate the day and time you ovulate, and plan to be together. Even the most fertile couple in the world has only a 20 percent chance of conceiving when they've done it at exactly the right moment under perfect conditions.

We have all heard our share of funny stories about the elaborate planning friends and relatives have had to undergo in order to get together on the right day at the right time. Couples have been known to plan a sudden stomachache so they could leave their jobs at the prescribed time and meet in a hotel room to have sex.

Sally had been taking her temperature every morning for three, maybe four months. We're on a schedule, you know. Well, one Sunday, I'm at my buddy's place. The phone rings. It's Sally. She's psyched, sure this is the moment. So, I grab my coat and run out, telling the guys I have to make a house call. They had to know what was going on. I was amazed I was up to the job.

Now, not everybody has to go this far, but don't be surprised if you find yourselves checking your calendars to make sure you can both be in the same place at the same time. And, don't be surprised if this pressure—even when it doesn't affect your sexual performance—puts more than a little strain on your patience with each other.

THE PRESSURE IS ON

The way you deal with anxieties and pressure will undoubtedly be tested now. At times like these, people's personalities become very clearly defined and we all tend to see the worst in even the people we love the most. Issues you and your partner might never have had to face may suddenly surface. You're involved in probably your most stressful joint undertaking since planning your wedding.

Well, there's no time like the present to learn to cope with crisis together. Stop for a minute and think about how much pressure you're under—performance pressures, the pressure of dealing with your private fears and hopes, day-to-day life pressures, work pressures, the monthly pressure of waiting to see if you're pregnant. True, thinking about this won't lessen the pressure, but it will help you to regain your perspective and restore those feelings of love.

Pressure is a very complicated issue. It brings out aspects of your personality that your partner may have never seen before. And make no mistake, the way your partner deals with this crisis—the avoidance, denial, assumption of responsibility, self-blame, overreacting, and inflicting of guilt—is how they will deal with emotional crises in the future. Start working out good problem-solving and depressurizing techniques now.

Under pressure, it is very easy for the goal in your relationship to shift from the health and happiness of the couple to having a baby no matter what. It's important you find a healthy way to deal with this. If you both feel really under the gun—the job is driving you nuts, everything's too much for you, sex is too scheduled—talk, get it out in the open, and if it will help, forget about having a baby until next month.

WHAT'S YOUR SCHEDULE?

Even though you may both want a baby, you may also each have a different degree of investment in a child. And face it. You are both different people. You approach your problems differently, so it makes perfect sense that you'll have different attitudes toward beginning a family.

Lois is a control freak, although she'd kill me if she ever heard me say it. And, once she makes up her mind to do something, get out of her way. I'm a little more laid back. By her standards, totally disorganized. She really expected to conceive on the first try. When I warned her not to expect too much. Wow!

Right from the start, it's a good idea to reach an agreement on your approach and your time frame. Do you want to actively plan so that you're pregnant in three months, six months? Or do you just want to relax with it, simply stop using birth control and get pregnant sooner or later, whenever?

Throughout your life as a couple you will face other crises—where to live, how to deal with finances—but little compares to the upheaval created by the decision to have a baby. So much of one's ego is invested in getting pregnant. You are creating something that is totally of you and a reflection on you, and any reaction to the way it is done or the outcome of this event will have a strong impact on you.

That's why planning and talking about how you want to approach this situation will be so helpful. Be upfront about it. Let your partner know what you are thinking. He may be able to share thoughts with you that will ease your fears. Save yourselves the anxiety of doubting each other. It's an unnecessary burden to carry at an already emotionally loaded time. Getting uptight can do more than start a few very heated arguments. This anxiety can affect your sexual interaction, and actually inhibit ovulation, making it even more difficult for you to get pregnant.

None of us are mind readers, but almost all of us can become very unnecessarily paranoid. At a time like this, when so much can be read into the most innocent of actions, words can really help to reinforce your love for each other and your mutual commitment to having a baby. Talk. Talk. Talk.

THE BIOLOGICAL CLOCK IS TICKING

The pressure can be tough on most couples, but it's particularly gruesome for an older couple trying to have their first child.

BABS: I'd made a choice—career, stable marriage and my feet firmly on the ground before I even considered having a kid. Well, it took a little longer than I'd expected for things to fall into place. It took over a year for us to get pregnant. I was furious with myself and Glen. Every month I didn't get pregnant I'd tell myself it would never happen.

GLEN: We spent a lot of time telling ourselves it didn't really matter. We had a good life, a baby would only mess things up. But, it didn't work. I could understand how Babs felt. Every period was telling her time was running out.

A woman who wants a child, but has an eye on the clock, may panic and actually make her situation worse.

STUART: I thought I loved Beth and, in fact, had told her

so. But we had only known each other three months and suddenly I found myself all caught up in discussing marriage and children. I know Beth was worried about her age, but this pressure made me wonder if she was interested in a life with me or just looking for a father for her children.

BETH: All of a sudden I turned around and I was 39! I knew I wanted a home and family, but I thought it would happen in time. So I spent five years with Stanley, a loser, and then the last nine years building my career. Stuart and I hit it off right away. And truthfully at 45, what was he waiting for?

WHEN DO YOU CALL A DOCTOR?

Probably the best way to get pregnant is to just relax and go about it the way people have for thousands of years. Have sex throughout the month while staying mindful of your fertile periods. Then, have sex every other night during your prime time. For most people, this is the way it generally happens, and if you believe it will happen naturally for you, it most likely will.

Consulting a physician at this point may be somewhat premature and may create an anxiety that is unnecessary. However, everybody is different. If you have a history of medical problems or are an older couple trying for a first child, you might want to talk to your gynecologist right from the beginning. As a general rule, however, if after six months of careful trying, you are not pregnant, we recommend that you consult a physician.

Once you make that call, unfortunately, you may both experience a new and even more potentially damaging type of anxiety. Why aren't I pregnant? What's wrong with me?

What's wrong with him? What if I can't? What will happen to our marriage? At this point you may each be struggling with the private fear that you are the one responsible for not getting pregnant. Try very hard not to cast blame on yourself or your spouse, and don't pull back from intimate contact. You're both scared, so help each other.

I think in the back of a woman's mind she always has the silent question—can I get pregnant? And, I guess a man wonders if he can get her pregnant. Well, after a lot of indecision, Jim and I decided to go for it and I panicked. I was 42 and in all my years of being sexually active, I had never gotten pregnant—what if I couldn't? When I told Jim my fears, he told me that he had the same fears—about me! Well, it was amazing how my rage at his arrogance pulled me out my self-pity. How could he be so sure any problem wasn't his?

WHAT WILL THE DOCTOR DO?

Tests, tests, and more tests, starting with the most basic sperm counts and blood hormone levels. Approaching this medical probing and poking truly requires your mutual support. As much as we'd like to, none of us has any control over our basic physiognomy. Eating well and exercising mean almost nothing when it comes to fertility. It's all genetic. So no one can be blamed for what their body is or is not prepared to do.

Sarah and David had been trying to get pregnant for about eight months. Sarah had a history of minor gynecological problems, but had really hoped they wouldn't interfere with her ability to conceive. Before putting Sarah through an exhaustive series of expensive tests, her doctor decided to first rule out the possibility of any problems with Dan.

We were both a wreck. Dan and I went to the fertility lab for his test. He came to my doctor with me. I can't begin to tell you how guilty and hopeless I felt when the tests confirmed that I had a problem.

Like many women faced with these circumstances, Sarah began to experience feelings of inadequacy. Her femininity was threatened. She even worried that her husband might leave her for a woman who could give him a child.

How did they make it through? Through all the crying and the disruptive and sometimes painful medical work they talked. It was hard. They both felt extremely vulnerable, angry with what they couldn't control, and reluctant to face some of their deepest fears.

SARAH: Some days I didn't want to even look at Dan. I was so angry, felt such a loss. He'd be affectionate. I'd withdraw. Then he'd feel hurt. It was terrible. We needed each other so desperately, but we were both so afraid.

DAN: Our relationship was really strained for a while. You know, a little chilly. I didn't like it. But I also knew I'd probably be the one to get us talking. Sarah was too distraught.

As frightening as opening up might have been, the damage to their relationship would have been far greater had they not braved the tumultuous depths of their feelings. No matter what, your goal should always be to maintain and build your intimacy, faith, and commitment to yourselves as a couple.

BUT I WANT IT

Unfortunately, you can't and don't always get what you want. You may be able to accept that like an adult and go on about your life as you would at any other time, but it just doesn't seem to happen that way when it's something as supposedly natural as having a baby.

Don't be surprised if one or both of you reverts to some fairly negative childish behavior. You're not getting what you want. You feel you are far more deserving of a child than anyone else. It's very understandable that you may feel completely helpless, out of control, and want to lash out.

Try not to blow things out of proportion. It's very easy to act like a brat and be angry with your partner. There really is no one to blame, so don't run away with these paranoid ideas. Some women find themselves suspecting their partner doesn't really want a baby as much as they do and is unconsciously manipulating, sabotaging their sexual interaction. Let logic step in for a minute. This sabotage without your knowledge is physically impossible, and your reasonable side knows it.

Blame is a very complex issue. At the same time you're blaming your partner because his sperm don't swim fast enough or something equally ridiculous, you're also feeling very guilty about blaming him. The next emotionally destructive step is to shoulder that guilt, blame yourself, and begin to suspect that being denied a child is retribution for some prior sins.

WISH I HADN'T DONE THAT

Many women approaching pregnancy start rethinking their pasts. Worrying that perhaps they'd been too promiscuous, had an abortion, experimented with drugs, suffered from venereal disease, been jealous and resentful of others, or simply toyed with the idea that they didn't want children.

Your past may haunt you, but it's highly unlikely that it's rendered you infertile. The ability to conceive and carry out a pregnancy has more to do with your genetic and biological constitution than any other factor. Regardless of what you may believe are the most terrible sins ever committed, your inability to conceive is not some kind of divine punishment. None of us are saints. We all make mistakes, but some superior being is not keeping a fertility scorecard on you. The truth is that some people do hideous life-threatening things, sins far worse than you could ever imagine, and they do conceive and give birth to healthy children.

JANET: I would wake up in a sweat remembering a bad relationship I'd been involved in. Convinced I was being punished because ten years ago my lifestyle was a little too wild and a little too promiscuous.

Once again, if you're suffering with that sort of anxiety, it can only help to talk about it. Approach this with your spouse honestly, but intelligently. Spare your partner the gory details, unless of course, that's the crux of the problem. In any case, be delicate. Honesty is often touted as a boon to good communication in a relationship, but when misused, it can be extremely destructive. Beware the need to confess to clear your conscience at the expense of your partner. Will spilling the beans bring the two of you closer together, or will it lead to hurt feelings, accusations and anger?

If you can't handle dredging up the past and possibly threatening the future of your marriage, find someone else to hear your confession. This may be a good thing to discuss with your doctor. Obstetricians are not there to judge, and sharing your worries with a professional may both allay your fears and alert your doctor to important medical information.

THE 28-DAY COUNTDOWN

> *LUCY: We'd been trying for ten months. No luck. When I got my period that month, I just broke down. I cried like a two year old. Feelings—guilt, blame, anger—I was a mess. Nothing Steve did helped. His comforting words made me even angrier.*

Today, most gynecologists advise patients trying to get pregnant to assume they are if they've had sex at their most fertile time, and to avoid drinking, drugs, smoking, coloring your hair, and over-the-counter medicines. While this is very smart medical advice, it can be very difficult to deal with emotionally.

Hoping you're pregnant, wondering if you are, if you aren't, envisioning yourself sharing the good news with your spouse is about the only thing you'll be able to think about for those two weeks. The disappointment you will feel when you do get your period, therefore, is to be expected. And the longer you go on without getting pregnant the less tolerant you are likely to be of your husband's, "It's okay honey. It'll happen next month."

MARILYN: Before we started trying to get pregnant, I had always suffered from PMS, not too severe. I'd get a little cranky, sobby. Forget about what happened after six months without birth control. I was a monster.

Waiting to see if you're going to get your period or not is a tremendous stress. Feelings of anger, blame, and fear about your fitness to be a parent can overwhelm you.

WHY AREN'T I PREGNANT?

This may be a question to bring to your doctor, particularly if you're an older couple or if you've been trying for more than six months. At the same time as the two of you are examining your physical ability to procreate, don't forget to look at the psychological side as well—not only as individuals but also as a unit.

TAMIE: I was really surprised that I didn't get pregnant instantly. After all, I had gotten pregnant twice before when I was being careful. So Jerry and I talked it over and when we got around to talking about us instead of talking about having a baby, we finally realized the problem—we were still really angry with each other about something that had happened years ago. No wonder I couldn't get pregnant!

Obviously, not all cases of difficult conception are psychologically based, but it is an aspect that should not be overlooked. Emotional exhaustion, anger, too much to do and worries can all effect your ability. Don't be surprised if your doctor tells you—after exhausting all physical possibilities—to just relax.

WONDER WOMAN?

For many women it is really important that they get pregnant without any medical assistance. The desire for fertility carries with it many unrealistic expectations. It is not uncommon for people to feel that any physical imperfections they suffer from or any inadequacies they feel about themselves will be immediately corrected or negated by conceiving and giving birth to a child. The ego involvement in getting pregnant is unlike any other experience in life. It brings into question one's sexuality, one's sense of real adequacy as a person and overrides all other physical and emotional realities we have lived with since birth.

Once you decide you both want a child, you will get scared and worry about your ability to give your partner a gift more extraordinary than any other. Your fears that your spouse will reject you if you don't produce a child and your need to connect and become a family will intensify.

ROSE: When Alan and I learned that I would have to have surgery to remove a blockage in my uterus before I could get pregnant, I totally broke down. I was so upset. Everyone else I knew had done it naturally and easily. Why couldn't I be like everyone else? I was so furious I walked around cursing under my breath at every new mother and pregnant woman I saw. Alan laughed at me and was so loving, he made me feel okay.

WHAT IF YOU CAN'T CONCEIVE?

There's no question that this will be a difficult moment. For many people, unfortunately, this is reality. The important thing to remember here is that your relationship, the love that you share, can still grow and thrive. Don't cast blame. Don't harbor guilt. Now is the time to find strength in each other and to use the intimacy that brought you to this undertaking to help you through. Exchange ideas and feelings, morning, noon, and night. Cry, scream, stamp your feet if you want. Reinforce your love for each other, and let your partner know that the most important thing is the two of you. There are other ways to become parents. Talk to your physician, too. When the desire to have a child stems from a joint feeling to create something, to bring a healthy productive life into the world, it is appropriate for you to consider adopting a child. There are many children in the world in need of a loving mother and father.

There is no question that childbirth is one life experience to which nothing else can compare. But when you want a child, and you bring your adopted child home, your passion and love for that child will be as great as it if were your natural born child.

You may, however, feel that adoption is not for you. At this point you must discuss how you will go on without a child. Remember, many of the happiest couples are childless. There are adult pleasures you can share that having a child will only postpone or cancel. So, while you may never have a child, there are many wonderful things to share as a couple. After all, being a loving couple is your top priority.

STAGE 3

THE GOOD NEWS

Your period is two weeks late. You had a little spotting. Then nothing. You've been late before. But, well, this time you've got a feeling.

TO TEST OR NOT TO TEST

Today, it really isn't a question of having to wait a long enough time to be sure of an accurate result. Modern tests, even the tests you can buy at the drugstore, are so sensitive you can test on the first day of a missed period and get an accurate result. Bear in mind, however, that any over-the-counter test should be confirmed by a doctor's test.

So, it's not really a question of having to wait, but of how soon you want to know. Most doctors urge early testing to insure a healthy pregnancy and infant. Most women, particularly those who have been trying for a long time, test as soon as they're one or two days late. Still, there are some people who prefer not to know that they're pregnant, claiming it will only add to their anxiety.

JOAN: I sort of knew I wasn't getting my period, but I wasn't paying too much attention to it. It was only when I started getting pains in my breasts and noticed that they were enlarging that I went for a test. By then, I was already three months pregnant. And I was very happy to have gotten to that point. I didn't deal with all the anxiety so many of my friends suffered. Worrying about whether or not they'd lose their baby. I'd made it past that point. I'm a believer in denial as a survival technique. Maybe that's not always the best way to take charge of your life, but . . . .

Waiting three months is not the best way to deal with your pregnancy or to insure a healthy baby. And, it certainly isn't going to prevent a miscarriage or make it any easier for you to live through one. But then, the way we relate to having a child is the way we relate to everything else in the world. Joan is a woman who doesn't confront things head on but waits until events dictate what she should do. She was very fortunate that in her denial she didn't suffer any health or nutritional problems. She had always been health conscious, and was already eating a pretty balanced diet. She also wasn't a smoker and must have known she was pregnant on some level because she didn't drink and had abstained from using any over-the-counter drugs.

Unlike Joan, Arlene, a woman who weighs herself every day, counts her calories, keeps a budget, and goes for annual checkups, couldn't wait to find out if she was pregnant. She went for a test the first day after she missed her period. She and her husband were both anxiously and delightedly anticipating the words "your test is positive." Arlene called her husband from the doctor's office the minute she got the news.

ARLENE: Edward answered the phone and I just blurted, "I'm pregnant. I'm pregnant." I think that's all I said. He named a restaurant, picked a time to meet, and without saying another word, hung up. We had a great celebration.

THE REALITY FACTOR

Arlene and Edward reflect a couple who planned the pregnancy and for whom the goods news was truly good news. This isn't always the case. There are couples who plan the pregnancy, but surprisingly find the good news doesn't feel like such good news.

Before the news many couples can only envision parenthood as nothing more than a romantic adventure. As the reality of parenthood displaces the fantasy, one or both of you may be overcome by severe trepidation.

CHARLIE: There we were. Still undecided, but sitting in the doctor's office waiting for Bonnie to have her abortion. Suddenly, I knew. I wanted to have this baby. I grabbed Bonnie's hand and pulled her out of the office. She cried. So did I. I guess we had to face the worst before we could decide to go through with it.

If you've been wanting a baby for a long time, your certainty about your pregnancy may not be this extreme. However, if one of you is normally pessimistic and responds to any good news by focusing on the negatives or potential dangers, you'll probably be at your worst when you learn you are about to become a parent.

Of course, this isn't tons of fun for the partner who's overjoyed by the news. Don't despair. Your spouse does want a child, but simply needs more time to adjust to the idea. Try to understand and have some patience. But never, ever stifle your enthusiasm. Your pregnancy is good news for you and you should let everyone know that. Find someone to share your excitement. If you have a best friend or are close to a parent, call them. It will help you to express your feelings and give your partner the time to reach a point of acceptance and true delight with the news.

Often the person who initially gets excited, but then responds negatively to the good news is someone who cannot deny the long-term realities of having a child. If you both share some real anxieties about your future with a child, right now those feelings will assume a tremendous importance for the more anxious person. For example, the reality of becoming a one-income household may totally overwhelm your husband and leave him single-mindedly focused on searching for a solution to your money problems. You can help by talking things through. Your husband really isn't retreating into this anxious state just to be a pain or to reject the baby and spoil all your happiness. Some people simply can't balance what's positive against what's terrifying them. Since they put their fears first, there is no way they can experience the news that they are about to get what they hoped for as good news.

MARLENE: I knew Roger took things more seriously than I did, but he was taking all the fun out of my pregnancy. He was so unenthusiastic. It really hurt. Then one day I heard him talking to my father on the phone and I could tell he was really worried that he wouldn't be able to handle the responsibility of a baby and a wife. My heart broke for him. I outlined some plans for budgeting, taking care of the baby, and even going back to work after six months. Once I opened up for the first time, let him know he wasn't in this all alone, we started to talk about names for the baby.

THE WRONG TIME. THE WRONG PERSON.

There are times when the good news truly is bad news. Unfortunately, this was the case for Janet. She was twenty-one years old, not too terribly happy in her marriage, and pregnant. The first thing she thought about when she heard the news was that her life was over. She would be tied down to a child for at least eighteen years.

> *JANET: My God, I thought, I'll be so old by the time this baby is grown. But, as I drove home from the doctor's office I pushed the gloomy feelings out of my head. Looking back on it, I would have been smarter to accept this wasn't the right time for me. I shouldn't have put on an act, carried on like Howard and I could make it wonderful.*

Janet's husband, Howard, wasn't too delighted by the news either. Only 22 years old and not yet earning a salary that could support two people, never mind three, being a father was not on the top of his agenda. This was the beginning of a very difficult time for them.

Admittedly, this is an extreme example, but it is not an uncommon one. If your marriage is young, even if it seems perfect, the arrival of an infant will really disrupt your years of passionate, selfish love—those years you really need to learn about each other, bond, get into your rhythm as a couple, build some financial security, and establish the rules of your relationship. One or both of you may feel trapped, abandoned, or manipulated. Now some couples find the support they need, and they work things through. Others, however, are just not ready to have a child when one drops into their life unannounced.

Conflicting emotions are not the province of unplanned pregnancies alone. Even the happiest of couples experience fear, anger, and resentment toward each other once the euphoria of the announcement has passed and reality sets in. This is particularly true if one spouse was a little more uncomfortable right from the outset and now feels manipulated into having a child.

Happy twosome or not, it's important to be honest with your partner. Let your partner know your real feelings about the coming child. If you're feeling frightened that you can't handle life as a dependent, non-income earning mother, if you feel overcome by the sense that your life now has a lasting commitment, don't pretend to be feeling something you're not. The results can be disastrous. This is especially so in the case of a pregnancy that is unplanned and occurring at a less-than-perfect time for you to be starting a family. An unplanned pregnancy, actually any pregnancy, requires a lot of upfront, extremely honest and realistic discussion.

GOOD? BAD? IT'LL GROW ON ME?

So, in other words, the good news can be exactly that—good news for a couple who planned and hoped for a child. It can foster ambivalence when one partner is more anxious or less prepared for it. Or it can take you totally by surprise. As Mark, a twenty-eight-year-old architect and first-time father put it, "I was thrilled. I just didn't think it would happen so fast." With a little time, Mark did grow comfortable with his impending fatherhood. Most people do. Pregnancy does take nine months, and that's good for a lot of reasons. It gives you plenty of time to adjust to the idea of yourselves as parents and to cement your union as a couple.

BAD ENOUGH TO END THE PREGNANCY?

What do you do if the good news is unpleasantly surprising news because you didn't plan, or very bad news because you really don't want to have a child? However you feel about your pregnancy and what you're going to do about it must be openly discussed. Janet and Howard, for example, may not have been open enough in their discussion of how to handle her unplanned pregnancy. This isn't rare. Even the most open couples are very reluctant to confront either giving their baby up for adoption or having an abortion. This is a personal and highly emotional decision, one that should only be reached after extensive discussion and total agreement by both partners.

MARY: Chris and I were very clear about how we felt right from the start. We'd probably get married one day. Have children. The whole bit. But not now. I was only in my sophomore year of college. Chris was on his way to medical school. There was no way.

For Mary and Chris the decision to not have a baby was an easy one. Most of the time, however, one partner is clearer about the decision than the other. Some couples even violently disagree on this decision. The best resolution under these circumstances is to postpone having a child. The opportunity to be a parent will most likely arise again at a more propitious time.

Alice became pregnant right after Matthew graduated from college. They'd been dating for two years, but believed that a couple should live together married or otherwise for at least two or three years before bringing a child into the world. They didn't feel that they knew each other well enough and did not want to get married just because Alice was pregnant. Although Alice wanted to have the baby, she agreed to have an abortion and put off the marriage.

Many times when a couple can easily decide against having the child, it's because they really have no desire to have a child under any circumstances nor any deep desire to get married. No one can tell you what is right under these circumstances, but if all your feelings lead you to believe that having a baby is wrong for you, it's probably best to find an alternative. Toughing it out doesn't make anyone, including the child, happy. Many of the couples who settle for this option suffer and cause their children to suffer through many very difficult and personally damaging years. These are the marriages that most often end in divorce. Why? Because it is always difficult when the foundation of your relationship hasn't been properly laid.

GOOD ENOUGH TO GO IT ALONE

Sometimes a woman is so convinced that she wants a baby that she is willing to continue the pregnancy even if the father doesn't want any part of it.

DOROTHEA: Honestly? I don't think I was in love with Raoul when I got pregnant. It was an accident. We had only gone out five or six times. I only knew I wanted the baby. He said he would never marry me or live with me. But he had always wanted a child too and would share the responsibility.

RAOUL: I liked the idea of becoming a father. I was there for the delivery. Luis was so magnificent. I had to see as much of him as I could. I asked Dorothea to come and live with me. I never thought it would happen. But, it turned out, she was such a wonderful mother and wife, I fell in love. She finally agreed to marry me.

Dorothea and Raoul shared a happy ending. Certainly, the joy of a child can bring a couple closer, but any woman who decides to have a child should only do so because she's 100 percent certain she wants the child. Not every man will make the turnaround Raoul did.

I DON'T FEEL PREGNANT

Most women don't feel particularly pregnant when they receive the news. Some women feel a little bit like they have the flu, a little sensitive in the breasts—sort of like PMS. Even if your test comes back positive, you may still just feel like you're going to get your period. Blame it on your hormones. If your pregnancy is a healthy one these symptoms will pass.

Many women, particularly first-time mothers, want to see or feel physical evidence of their pregnancies. We have all heard so many old-wive's tales about how to know whether a pregnancy is a healthy one, whether you're having a girl or a boy, and on and on, that it's not surprising women want to look pregnant instantly. Feeling nothing different about their newly pregnant body can be very unsettling. Physical discomforts—vomiting, nausea, bloating, craving—are therefore taken by many women as a positive sign that there is no mistake, the pregnancy is real.

I was so happy to be pregnant. I'd waited so long. But I didn't feel any different. The only thing that did hurt me were my breasts. So every now and then, even at work, I'd take a little trip into the ladies room and unhook my bra.

Well my breasts would kill me and then I'd feel okay. Silly, maybe? But it helped me to relax.

On the other hand, some women are thrilled to still have their usual shape. For these women the knowledge that their body is soon to undergo a major change can be very unnerving. For many women body image is key to their identity—perhaps they have always been slim, perhaps they were once overweight and now struggle to maintain their figures—and gaining weight to have a baby can truly disrupt their sense of who they are.

WHOSE BODY IS THIS ANYWAY?

I'd never been a pound overweight in my life. I was a skinny kid and liked the fact that I was flat chested, sort of model-skinny. Even before I'd gone for my test, I was suspicious. I needed a bra. That was an all-time first for me. I freaked. When I got the test results, I was thrilled and then totally panicked by the realization that soon I'd be a little chub.

This is a difficult adjustment for many women. Women who have had to struggle to stay thin worry that they will be unable to control their eating, blow up, and then be unable to lose the weight after the baby is born. If you have suffered with a weight problem, talk to your doctor right away and have him recommend a diet. Weight Watchers has an extremely good program. If your doctor thinks you're a healthy candidate, join. It will provide a healthy, hearty, and calorie-controlled diet and a tremendous support system to guide you through even your worst potato chip and donut cravings.

MEN ARE STARING AT ME

Well, it's never fun to be gawked at on the street, but this does seem to happen to a lot of pregnant women. You barely look pregnant, maybe just a little bustier, and every strange man on the planet seems to know. How do they know, and why are they looking at me? Our society glorifies the skinnier, more boyish female body type—at least when it comes to fashion. For many people, usually men, a more rounded, softer female body is beautiful. You may feel uncomfortable with your new fullness but you are actually developing a more voluptuous, very female body. Don't hate the lookers; look back at them. You'll see pleasure and approval in their eyes. Just as (almost) everybody loves a cute baby, almost everybody loves an attractive pregnant woman. She is carrying the miracle of life. Relish your pregnancy, recognizing it as an opportunity to experience another kind of womanliness that indeed is highly valued in all cultures.

WHO DO YOU TELL? WHEN?

Once you and your partner have shared the good news with your obstetrician, the question is when do you share the good news with others. Whom do you tell, and how do you tell? There is a common superstition that urges you wait at least twelve weeks for the fear of putting any kind of evil eye on your pregnancy. This is partly based on the medical reality that most miscarriages occur in the first twelve weeks, and partly due to the belief that you shouldn't admit to having had sex until you absolutely have to.

Some couples don't, however, wait the twelve weeks, particularly if they've been trying to get pregnant for a long time and are more than a little excited about the news.

At 40 I was dying for a baby. I certainly wasn't going to wait to share the good news. We told everybody. I just felt, well, if something does go wrong, there's nothing I can do about it. I'd rather have the people close to me know what I'm going through—good or bad—than trying to keep a big secret.

A miscarriage is a terrible, sorrowful experience, but you should feel no shame or guilt should you be so unfortunate as to have a miscarriage. If you can handle the possibility that you may have to come back and tell people that things did not go as well as you'd expected, then there is absolutely no reason not to share your good feelings before the danger period has passed.

There are some definite benefits to sharing your joy very early. It's always easier to sustain whatever difficulties you may endure when you've got people to help you. First of all you won't be parading around with a stiff upper lip harboring the secret that you're pregnant. You will be surrounded by people who understand why you're sick in the morning, upset or moody, and they can help. In fact, this may be the perfect time to get together and pow-wow with other couples who've been through a pregnancy. It will help you to understand some of what's happening to you, and what to expect. This will help the two of you to grow closer as you face this new stage in life together.

HOW WILL YOUR FRIENDS TAKE IT?
Like we've said before, how your friends will respond has everything to do with how they think a child would affect their lives, their own childhood, their own parenting experience, and your relationship with them. It probably has

nothing to do with how your decision will affect you.

Some friends may feel that you're too young for the responsibility. Now, you're really the only two who can answer that. If you do find yourselves believing there may be some truth in their comments, now's the time to deal with it. If you really want this baby, establish a support system that can help you through the tough spots. Find other couples with children and, most important, get comfortable with the new reality you will face.

Older couples also can suffer at the hands of less-than-mature friends. Even though many couples are taking to parenting much later in life, there is still some shock (at least among small-minded people) when a couple who seems to have it all—love, career, money, the good life—announces they're about to have a baby.

Sabrina and Joe were both 40 when Sabrina got pregnant. They felt blessed. It had taken them years to realize they wanted a child and quite a long time to conceive.

SABRINA: Becky and Howard were our best friends. They had two teen-aged boys. We'd watched their kids grow up, shared a lot of their anguish and pride. That's what made it so upsetting, I guess. We told them and they just blurted out, "What are you nuts?"

JOE: At first, Sabrina started explaining our decision to them. I stopped her. I was furious. Becky spouted some little platitude about how we had the perfect marriage, kids are so tough. You know. I thanked her for the kind afterthought, got our coats, and we left.

HELLO MOTHER. HELLO FATHER.

How to tell your parents or when to tell them, of course, has to do with who your parents are and what sort of relationship you share. Most couples are delighted to tell their parents because most parents are delighted to hear that they are going to be grandparents. Many mothers-to-be say that the closest, most emotional moment they have ever shared with their mothers was when they announced they were pregnant.

Once again, how they take the news has everything to do with their parenting experiences. If it was a good experience, they'll probably be delighted. If not, well . . . And just as you like to think of yourself as young and vital, so do your parents. If the potential grandparents have negative feelings about their own aging process, do not consider themselves old enough for the rocking chair, they may not be happy to be grandparents. It may be best to wait until their reaction will be easier for you to take.

It may also be tough to tell parents with whom one or both of you has some unsettled business. The news of the pregnancy may exacerbate your problems or push you into an untimely discussion or resolution of these issues.

Most parents do respond with joy, pride, and love. Their baby has grown up. They've done a good job and are about to be blessed with a second chance at totally selfless love. However, you know your parents better than anyone else, and if you think they might freak, you and your spouse should decide how you will deal with them.

PEGGY: I was an obnoxious child. My mother's nickname for me was "her cross to bear." She was always telling me how she hoped someday I would have kids that tortured me the way I did her. I was terrified to tell her I was pregnant—

actually terrified that my baby would be just like me. I didn't want her to say, "Now you're pregnant to get it all back."

DENNIS: I called Peg's parents. They both broke into tears. They were so happy. Her mother started carrying on about how Peggy had been such a wonderful child. That her baby would be perfect. I guess happiness can cause amnesia.

If your parents are particularly anxious or tend to hover over you, you may want to delay the announcement. Give yourselves enough time to get your lives in order before they attempt to walk in and take over—instructing you in health care, choosing your obstetrician, buying a new apartment, planning junior's college education. This anxious parent may also start worrying about how you're waking up every morning, how you're crossing the street. They may strongly suggest that you quit your job and stay home for nine months. If you weren't a nervous wreck before, this type of parental intervention is likely to push you over the edge. So think of yourself first, get comfortable about the news, and then share it. As a couple, plan the approach you'll take to parents and friends, and stick together.

My mother-in-law was great in a crisis—and every event qualified as a crisis! Jonathan and I agreed that we would present a united front in all our dealings with her. We would never tell her anything negative nor argue with her advice. We were completely confident that we would do exactly what we wanted to do after she left. This could never have worked if we hadn't planned, or if I had the least insecurity about Jonathan's allegiance to me.

This should really be a time for you and your husband

to share your closeness without pressure to do anything. Actually, having a baby begins by just sharing the good news with your spouse, your family and close friends, enjoying and engaging in the fantasy and excitement of the coming baby. Since you've accepted that this is the right time to have a baby, create the right emotional atmosphere, too.

FINAL EXAM

DO YOU HAVE THE RIGHT DOCTOR?

Your doctor may have done a smashing job of doing your pregnancy test, but is this the physician you want to trust with the health and well-being of your unborn child? If you're not comfortable with your doctor, now is the time to find someone new. Look for the same qualities in a doctor that you do in a spouse—acceptance, understanding, caring, and excellent credentials. But remember, no matter how famous or brilliant he is, it won't help you if you don't feel comfortable and cared for.

DO YOU HAVE A GAME PLAN?

Sit down together and start listing the things you both feel will need adjusting to smoothly integrate a baby into your lives. Will you have to move? Where? Who will stay at home? What will the delivery be like? Believe me, you've got plenty to think and talk about—and talk you must.

ARE YOU BOTH SPEAKING YOUR HONEST FEELINGS?

Now is not the time to grin and bear it or keep things to yourself. Make a pledge to work on your communication skills. Learn to keep close and open, how to express the positive and negative, and how to be honest without being a beast.

HAVE YOU TALKED ABOUT FINANCES?

No, don't do it as soon as the test comes back positive, but now's the time to develop a plan and face reality. Talking about money is never fun, so ease into it.

ARE YOU SHOWING EACH OTHER HOW IN LOVE YOU ARE?

Most important. It's always easier when your love for each other is a big part of your everyday life.

STAGE 4

THE FIRST TRIMESTER

No matter how long you've been anticipating this pregnancy, nor how many stories you've heard about morning sickness and first trimester physical changes, nothing can really prepare you for what may actually occur when you're at the mercy of your hormones.

I FEEL ATROCIOUS

Once you've enjoyed the glorious rush of excitement at becoming pregnant and shared the good news with those few people whom you've chosen to tell, the good news may feel like bad news that first morning you're hunched over, retching in the bathroom. The first trimester is not fun. As any woman who has survived all nine months will tell you, this is the worst part of being pregnant. Your body is undergoing a cataclysmic hormonal readjustment, and no matter what you feel you want to do, during this twelve-week period, your hormones are going to make the rules.

THE TRUTH ABOUT MORNING SICKNESS

This unpleasant phenomenon doesn't occur with every pregnancy, and it doesn't always happen first thing in the morning. You might suffer from afternoon, evening, or midnight sickness—or nothing at all. Don't listen to all those old-wive's tales. Suffering from morning sickness is no indication of whether or not you're going to have a healthy baby. Whether or not you will be vomiting through the first three months of your pregnancy has everything to do with how your body reacts to the hormone adjustments you are going through and nothing more.

THE BEST YOU CAN DO IN A BAD SITUATION

Always follow your doctor's diet. Do your best to get all the essential vitamins and minerals, and don't make a pig of yourself. Overeating will only make you more uncomfortable.

Listen to your body and it may start to listen to you. You will slowly learn what you can and can't eat, and what the best time is for a meal. If you really can't face the sight of a bowl of cereal the minute you crawl out of bed, wait a while. You can eat breakfast an hour or two after you wake up. You don't have to eat by the clock. Just eat what you're supposed to at the times your body can handle it best.

I'M SO SO SO SO TIRED

Unless you have already experienced one pregnancy, there is no way to explain the depletion of energy you will feel in the first trimester. The exhaustion is profound. You may try your best to cope, but chances are good that you won't be operating at peak performance. Chatting with a friend may be too exhausting, so just imagine how zonked you will feel after working, cleaning, cooking, and completing all your other daytime chores. Some things will naturally take a slide. This inability to live up to their own high standard turns some women into outright dragons and bewilders others. Don't panic; this is not permanent. You will return to the land of the living in about twelve weeks, but right now you've got to take it slow.

Not surprisingly, the people who have grown accustomed to your super-woman routine may get a little annoyed with you. If they don't know you're pregnant or have never been pregnant themselves, your behavior will seem somewhat unusual. If your usual eight-hour work day leaves you in need of a two-hour nap before dinner, your hungry husband and family may feel a little disappointed. So, don't be surprised when people get a little short-tempered about all the adjustments they're having to make in their lives. Undoubtedly, this apparent selfishness may make you furious, but it's important to remember they just don't have a clue as to how you are feeling right now.

PHYLLIS: I guess their complaining did upset me, but the truth is, I was just too tired to care. I just ignored my son and husband when they'd start moaning that they couldn't find this or that. I'd go into the bedroom and close the door. But the disorganization finally got to me, too. Tired as I was I finally saw that the house was a mess and so were they. I tried to help, but I didn't have the energy. Finally, I got smart and hired our neighbor's housekeeper. She'd come around and help out for a few hours every evening. Not so amazingly, I was less tired.

For those extremely independent women who are

driven to overachieve, this sudden dip in energy may also put their self-image into question. And this can result in some very illogical and ugly behavior. Their frustration may transfer itself into anger at their husbands. They may resent him because he gets to have a baby without going through the agony of pregnancy. This makes a lot of sense, right? Wrong.

DAN: I couldn't understand why Penny was acting like it was my fault for "knocking her up." We had both planned it after all.

PENNY: Dan was acting like being tired was my fault. I was screaming about how much agony I was in. One time, when we were going out, I really heard us and burst out laughing. Our argument was totally ridiculous—just frustrations. That was when I hit upon the idea of asking him to cater to me. I asked him to bring me little presents, indulge my food cravings.

DAN: I felt much better when Penny started to let me know what I could do to make her feel better. At least I was sharing in her ordeal.

You both wanted this baby. Now, you are taking the first step in adjusting to its arrival. It's rough. After all, this is probably the first time in your lives that you have had to adjust to circumstances that have everything to do with the two of you and over which you have no control. While some couples reach an easy peace with all of this, others find it a bit more difficult. How you handle these early months is a good test of how well you will adjust to the arrival of the child.

THIS ISN'T THE MAN I MARRIED

CAROL: Larry and I had a wonderful urban existence. After work we'd meet for a leisurely dinner at a restaurant. We'd share our day over a glass of wine and a good meal, head home to watch television or read. That ended real fast. Larry was still itching to go out. But I was lucky to make it home and crawl into bed after work. The last thing I wanted was a meal in a restaurant.

RESOLVING PREGNANCY ADJUSTMENT PROBLEMS

What are the feelings that are keeping you from enjoying this pregnancy? When Larry examined his avoidance he realized that he associated Carol's behavior with illness, and that revolted him. He was then able to realize he was associating his wife's symptoms with his terrible memory of the years he had spent in bed recuperating from a serious childhood illness.

What can you do to overcome these feelings? Larry discovered that inviting friends home after work instead of going out made Carol feel better and helped him differentiate her feelings from his childhood illness.

LARRY: I think I really caused Carol a lot of pain. I just couldn't stay home in the beginning. I'd meet friends after work for dinner and roll in about 9:00 or 10:00 P.M. She'd be in tears. She was going through this for the both of us. I guess I couldn't handle the reality of it all. I should have been home with her. I just didn't make the adjustment too easily.

One thing that can help both of you through this is to

be reassured that what everyone tells you is true. The ills of the first trimester will pass. You will be amazed at how the fatigue lifts, and you can once again enjoy a normal life. Your pregnancy has not destined you to be an invalid for the next nine months. It is only in very rare cases that women are forced to take to their beds for their entire pregnancy.

WHAT HAVE WE DONE?

Long before you look pregnant you will experience the physical changes that force you to face the reality that a baby is on the way. Don't be surprised if that ambivalence you experienced during the planning stages resurfaces with a new intensity. Everything you've dreamed about is real now. What if it's not what you expected? What if you can't manage it? What if everything goes wrong? Will you be a good parent and financially able to sustain this child for the next twenty years? These are all very real fears, so don't be shocked if they leave you feeling uncertain that you want a child. What's essential is that you verbalize this ambivalence to each other.

Under most circumstances talking will help you both to feel less isolated and to put things in perspective. There is, however, one exception to our recommendation for total openness. And that is if your ambivalence or fear will cause your partner irreparable pain. Perhaps you're worried that your child will look like or have a personality trait you don't particularly care for in your husband or his family. First of all, this is an irrational idea. If you don't like the way your spouse looks, why are you even with him? Think for a minute about what the real problem is here. Often feelings like this are just a mask for other fears. In any case, it is far better to share these confused and very negative anxieties about your spouse with a friend or a counselor. They can tell you how ridiculous they are and help you to sort out your real concerns.

UNPLANNED AND VERY UNCERTAIN

If this is an unplanned pregnancy and you're both convinced this is not the time to be having a child, it is imperative that you talk and reach a mutual plan of action very early on. You do have the option of abortion, depending on your personal beliefs, or giving your baby up for adoption. But no matter what course you choose to take, this must be a joint decision. Neither of you should feel that you've been forced into something you will resent for the rest of our life.

LILLI: Jack said that he would leave me if I didn't have an abortion. I knew I wanted the baby. When I told my parents, they were unbelievable. They offered to support me and the baby! Six months after Lonnie was born I met Kent. He loved Lonnie as if she were his. I don't know where Jack is, but things have worked out beautifully for me.

How you deal with the ambivalence about your pregnancy reflects how you live your life overall. Some people deal with their ambivalence by ignoring the pregnancy. In fact, my patient Susan did such a wonderful job of ignoring her pregnancy that she never even bought maternity clothes until the seventh month, when the need to put on a bathing suit forced her into a maternity shop. Ironically, in Susan's case, the fact that she chose to ignore her pregnancy, other than to make monthly or bimonthly visits to her doctor, allowed her to escape all of the typical first trimester symptoms. It was her husband who suffered all the anxiety, and just as in tribal groups, he even had morning sickness.

WHAT'S SUPPOSED TO HAPPEN NOW?

In the beginning of their pregnancy, many men and women need confirmation that everything is going just fine. So, they naturally ask their friends about symptoms they had and how they may have felt at this time in their pregnancy. While this helps to take the mystery and uncertainty out of the first months, you shouldn't assume that your friend's experience will be yours. In other words, don't anticipate. Don't fall prey to "medical students' disease" and develop every symptom that you hear about, or worry that you're not developing symptoms that other people have. When it comes to symptoms, no two pregnancies are the same, even for the same woman.

In fact, many women have no unusual first trimester symptoms. Some women even claim that they didn't know they were pregnant for the first four months. That may seem incredible, but it can be true, particularly for women who commonly miss periods without being pregnant. Of course, the other possibility is that these women did not want to face their pregnancy and ignored the symptoms, thereby declaring themselves symptom-free.

HORMONES DO THE FUNNIEST THINGS

GREG: Eileen was a wreck during the Olympics. Every time one of those really sappy patriotic television commercials— you know the beer spots that talk about greatness—would air, she'd cry, "Oh, Greg, isn't that beautiful." I thought she was losing it. My wife doesn't even cry at funerals. Truth-fully, I kind of like this emotional side—when she's not yell-ing at me, of course.

You may find yourself crying at commercials, being overly sensitive to the way your husband kisses you good night, or the way your mother says hello on the telephone. This heightened sensitivity is normal for many women during the first trimester.

WHO'S MORE IMPORTANT

You're not the only one going through changes right now. Your husband is experiencing some major upheavals of his own. Although he may have been part of the concep-tion, he is now very separate from the pregnancy. The sense of not totally being a part of your connection with this developing child can be disturbing for your husband and put a strain on your relationship.

MATT: The way Cassie devoured maternity clothes it looked like she was planning to stay pregnant for the next ten years. She was so caught up in her pregnancy she spent more time discussing it with her girlfriends than with me.

CASSIE: Matt conveniently forgot how excited he gets when he has a new account and how much time he spends going over the details with his colleagues—not with me. He does have a point though. In my usual take-charge fashion I've been zipping along and have forgotten to include him.

Many husbands feel a little resentment about the very private and personal relationship between you and the growing child. Up until this point he has been the one person you've been the most intimately involved with. Now someone else is coming between you. Despite your physical misery and your heightened emotions, it is extremely important that you include your husband in every aspect of your pregnancy. Share with him some of the physical feelings that you are experiencing. Let him know how you're dealing with the morning sickness. Let him know what the doctor says. Bring him to some doctor's visits. Include him in the physical development of the fetus. Spend some time reading books on what is happening and will happen at different points in your pregnancy.

Get into the habit of always speaking in the *we*. When you speak to your husband about the baby, speak in terms of *we*. When you speak to friends about your pregnancy, speak in the *we*—*we're* going to have a baby. This will go a long way to reassuring him that you are still very much an intimate couple who have created something wonderful together. It will establish that he is not an outsider, but still the most important person to you.

YOU DON'T TOUCH ME ANYMORE

Don't be surprised if your husband gets a little physically standoffish, particularly if this is your first pregnancy. He may be frightened of hurting you. He has no idea what's going on inside of you and may worry that any physical contact could cause you and the baby distress.

GWEN: Barry was always the first one in bed. He used to read or we'd chat while I got undressed. Well, all that changed. He'd go stone silent and just stare at my body. He'd look at my breasts, then my belly with this expression on his face that was like, "Well, what's going on? I don't see a baby, yet."

FRAGILE, HANDLE WITH CARE

During the first trimester, there is a tendency to feel that you should treat yourself like you're made of glass, that your pregnancy has made you fragile. Yes, you are carrying something precious that is nurturing inside of you, but you are not an invalid nor are you physically damaged or sick.

You can and should continue normal activities. By all means, adjust to your physical changes. This is not the time to take up rock climbing, but don't be a sissy either. Let your body determine its own schedule. If you feel that you just can't make it to your exercise class because you're exhausted, don't push yourself. And, don't feel guilty about needing that hour to nap. You'll spring back into form during the second trimester.

Your physical capabilities during your first trimester depend on two things: first, what you've done before, and second, how well your pregnancy is beginning. If you are having a difficult first trimester and are considered at any risk, it is likely that your doctor will recommend abstaining from any heavy physical activity—exercise, shifting furniture, carrying anything heavy—or even constant bedrest. Again, it is important that you know your body and listen to your doctor.

If your pregnancy is a healthy one, you should be able to do everything you did before without harming yourself. As a matter of fact, stopping a well-established exercise routine could cause you anxiety—all that extra time with nothing to do could quickly become time you spend worrying about your pregnancy. The truth is that if you are involved in a healthy pregnancy, it will run its course no matter what you do, and if you're likely to miscarry, you will miscarry no matter what you do. This may sound like harsh advice, but a miscarriage truly is nature's way of taking care of what is not a healthy fetus. If you are involved in an unhealthy pregnancy, it really is best to try again.

THIS ISN'T ME

While you're not supposed to turn into a couch potato, frightened to move, you do now have a larger purpose in life. Your body is now there to nurture and protect this fetus, and you will begin to establish a physical and psychological link with your developing child. You may find yourself shielding your rounding belly with your hands to protect your stomach from people bumping into you on the street.

Your body has a new purpose now. You are supporting a new life, and your body wants to protect this life no matter what. This new protectiveness and sense of purpose also affects your interest in things other than having this baby. A lot of pregnant women who have high-powered jobs have been known to suddenly become very laissez-faire about work. Being on time for a meeting now seems less important than having an extra minute to talk to your doctor. A patient of mine summed it up by saying, "I don't seem to care about anything but having my baby." Priorities definitely shift now, including your interest in sex.

SEX? WHAT'S SEX?

You may have been a regular little passion flower four weeks ago, but you're definitely wilting now. When it comes to sex, your body is once again setting the limits. The first trimester and the last month are the only times when sex can place the fetus at risk. If you have no libido, it's simply because your hormones are taking control.

> *EVA: I could see that Dave was disappointed but I just didn't feel any sexual desire. I really loved him and I felt very good about being pregnant, but I just had no desire for anything more than hugging and holding.*

Though you may have no desire for sex, this may not be the case for your husband. This is when flexibility becomes an even more essential ingredient in your marriage. As your sexual interaction goes through these temporary changes, you must both be willing to adapt to the other person's needs. Holding and hugging and kissing may be all that you desire, but your husband is still living with a normal male sex drive. It may be necessary for you to satisfy him, manually or orally, even at a time when you have a lack of interest. It's very important that you communicate to your husband that your lack of sexual interest is not a rejection of him. Many a man worries that now that you're pregnant you are no longer interested in him. It's very important that you reassure him and yourself that this is not a loss of interest in him or a preference for the child over the father.

Your sex drive will return. It comes back in the second trimester. Everything comes back. Life returns to normal after the first three months. You can look forward to at least five good months of carefree sex. Of course, sex will be curtailed again toward the end of the pregnancy.

WHAT, ME WORRY?

Pregnancy is a time when men and women lose a lot of sleep worrying about things that, unfortunately, they have no control over. You worry about your past and whether or not anything you've ever done in your life could possibly hurt your child. You worry about coming in contact with people who may be carrying tonsillitis, measles, or any communicable diseases.

You worry about environmental influences. You worry about nature and the threat of birth defects and disability. Unfortunately, you have no control over many of these things. These risks come with pregnancy, but with good prepregnancy health, prenatal care, advanced medical diagnostics, abstinence from alcohol, drugs and other substances known to be dangerous to a fetus, you can minimize the risk.

If you know that you are in a high risk group (that is, if you are forty or have a family history of birth defects or serious health problems), then caution is in order. You should by all means talk to your doctor about amniocentesis. And if you believe there are serious genetic considerations, look into genetic counseling as well.

Fortunately, few infants are born handicapped or are atypical births. Try and remind yourself of this, and keep your own good health in mind. When you suffer from these worries, the best thing to do may be to have your spouse offer reassurance. You don't really need someone to agree with you now. Comfort and reassurance that everything is going to be okay is the best medicine a spouse can provide.

GENA: I would wake up in a sweat every night. I'd toss, turn, punch the pillows, and then Les would wake up, too. Suddenly I'd be asking him if he thought the case of the measles I'd had twenty years ago could have caused permanent genetic damage. At first, we'd discuss things logically, accepting certain realities and assuring each other we could handle whatever nature dealt us. Then we'd both reassure each other that everything was fine. There was nothing wrong with our baby. Then we'd fall back to sleep.

Even though you may both suspect that you're being superficially reassuring, believe it or not, this behavior works. Don't try figuring it out. Just keep doing it.

FACING NEW REALITIES

Even this early in your pregnancy you will notice a readjustment in the number and type of responsibilities you each share. It happens to every couple, and it's not always the easiest adjustment to make. If you work, you long to keep your independent, career-driven image intact, but the physical changes that are occurring force you to face the facts. There are few or no women who can deliver a baby and head back to work two weeks later. What you are experiencing now is the first indication that your role in the family and in the world is about to change.

What will life be like when you're no longer a wage earner? What will your role in your marriage be? Will you become a traditional housewife, a dependent instead of an equal? These questions can be very unsettling, and it's best to confront them early on.

Often times, the feelings and expectations you have about motherhood are a direct reflection of the feelings conveyed to you by your mother and her experience. If your biggest fear is that you will become an insignificant housefrau, that your husband will see you in a demeaning light, chances are good your mother suffered from these problems. It's important for you to distinguish her fears from the reality of your own experiences and relationship.

Keep an eye out for danger signs. Don't assume that all the responsibilities of your child and your home should now fall on your shoulders. We are all victims of some very traditional conditioning, and it's easy for any one of us to revert to behavior that we're not comfortable with simply because it's the only role model we've seen. You're not supposed to become Donna Reed just because you are soon to be a mother. Think about the person you were when you and your husband fell in love and the person you were just weeks before when you didn't know you were pregnant. It's important that you don't abandon that person. It's key to your individual happiness and the future of all of you as a functioning family unit.

DONNA: When I realized what I was doing I was shocked. It was as if, upon learning that I was going to be a mother, I became a mother—unfortunately, my mother. As if I had been sent backward in a time machine. I was convinced that my husband was acting just like my father had—out with his friends, insensitive to me at home alone, waiting for him.

DUANE: Fortunately, Donna is a little saner than her mother. She saw what was happening between us. I pointed out that I hadn't changed anything—she had—and made some pretty crazy assumptions besides. Like, why was she rushing home right after work when she knew I got out two or three hours later than she does? Why wouldn't she meet me in the city for dinner out? It was like she was preparing for the misery of motherhood.

LIFE WITH MOTHER-TO-BE

If you or others accuse you of exhibiting uncharacteristic behavior, take a minute to think about all the changes you're going through. Ask yourself these questions. Your answers may reveal some feelings you aren't aware of.

1. How do you feel about your mother?
2. Do you have a clear vision of yourself as a mother and wife?
3. Do you include your husband in your fantasies about life with baby?
4. Can you handle the body change?
5. Do you feel that your pregnancy demands that you now act like an angel or a saint?
6. Do you want to keep your job?
7. Do you feel you must be super mom?
8. How do you feel about your father?
9. Do you have a clear vision of your husband as a father?
10. Do you think its the same as his idea?
11. Do you feel you must now change who you are to become a mommy?

HUSBANDS HAVE WORRIES, TOO

At the same time you're fearing the change in your status as an equal and a financial participant in your marriage, your husband will very likely be fearing the same thing. He may be very comfortable with the fact that you earn a healthy income, and he may depend on that income, as you both do, to sustain a good standard of living. He must now face the realization that he will soon be the sole provider not only for two adults but also for a very dependent infant.

In today's economic climate, this is an awesome pressure even for the most well-paid man. Your husband could really use some help. While morning sickness and midnight fears are exhausting, you must take the time to sit down together and outline the financial realities you will face after the baby is born. This gives you plenty of time to sort out a plan of action and eliminate the likelihood of either one of you being surprised when there just isn't as much money as there used to be.

WHAT AM I—DOGMEAT?

Money is probably not the only worry your husband is facing right now. He may, in fact, be worrying about losing his relationship with you. Pregnancy is a time when our society really focuses its attention on the mother-to-be, and your husband can feel very excluded. Many men experience a sense of loss early on in the pregnancy. The developing baby seems to be taking on more importance than your relationship. It is the focus of your attention and discussion, and actually controls your physical and emotional life. Your husband could, therefore, easily draw the conclusion that he is no longer an important part of your life.

TALK TO HIM. LISTEN TO HIM.

You love this man or you wouldn't be having this

child. Now you must communicate that, but not by simply telling him you love him and assuring him that everything is fine. Sit down and get him talking. Listen to his fantasies about what life is going to be like when the baby comes, his hopes, the things you both want to happen for the three of you in the future. In other words, just as you shouldn't abandon the person you were before your pregnancy, you shouldn't leave your husband to just soldier on alone while you play the role of the expectant mother instead of wife.

As much as Ted said he wanted a child and was really looking forward to the baby, he felt totally lost during the first trimester.

TED: I felt like now that Joan was pregnant, my job was done. All I could do was sit back and watch her belly grow.

JOAN: I felt so sorry for Ted. When he first heard the news, he was ready to run out and buy a football. Then, he seemed to be so lonely. It was my responsibility to keep him involved in my pregnancy. So, every night, we'd read together. You know, the books your doctor recommends during pregnancy. He'd rub my belly. Then we felt like a family. Not a mother-to-be and a stranger living in the same house.

IT'S ALL MY FAULT

In addition to feeling left out, your husband may also be feeling very guilty right now. Many men really can't bear seeing their wife in pain or discomfort and want very much to cure what ails them. Of course, they can't do that, so the man who can't save you from your suffering may begin to feel very helpless—which can easily lead to guilt if he makes the association that what you're feeling is his fault since he got you pregnant. Now, this is blatantly illogical, but so are many emotions, and if you suspect your husband may be experiencing this response, remind him that he didn't do this all on his own.

Involve your husband in your aches and their relief. It will help him to feel part of what you're going through, part of your cure, even if you start to tease him about being your Florence Nightingale. Let him help you keep track of what you're supposed to be eating and when. On the days that you don't feel too good, don't be a martyr and cook dinner. Ask your husband to cook one of his favorite meals that night. Helping in these really tangible ways may help him feel that he is really contributing something to the health and well-being of your baby. And, perhaps even more important, maintain the egalitarian interchange.

Just as some husbands feel left out, there are some husbands who get so involved in the pregnancy that they, too, develop first trimester symptoms. It's an old joke, but it does happen, and that's when it's your turn to be supportive and sympathetic. If you husband feels nauseous in the morning, you can't disregard this. It's his way of saying that he wants to be identified with your pregnancy. Love him for it, even when you're bursting to get in the bathroom, too.

LIFE WITH FATHER-TO-BE

Now that Romeo is about to be transformed into Ward Cleaver, you may find the adjustment a little rocky. What follows is a list of potential hot issues for the new father-to-be. As your pregnancy progresses, of course, new issues and complications will present themselves. This is just a guide to get you through the first upheaval.

1. *A man's relationship with his father will definitely affect his image of himself as a father.*

   You may feel your child will feel the same way about you that you feel about your father—and you may not feel too good about that. If your father is dead, you may feel sadness, anger , or total isolation. If you had no role model, you may truly panic about your ability to father. After all, you don't know what you're supposed to do.

2. *A man may worry that he can't make it as a super dad.*

   Today, fathers work longer and harder than ever before. At the same time that the financial pressure heats up, so does the emotional pressure. You don't want to be the kind of father that collapses in a heap at the end of the day, but you also worry about whether you'll have the energy to nurture a demanding child.

3. *Being the sole support of your family is tough.*

   Bring home the bacon, be responsive, balance your time at work with your time at home. Build a career while enjoying a family. It's tough. You'll need a lot of emotional support, so it's a good idea to start talking about this right now.

4. *Most men love to be nurtured and pampered by their wives. How will you handle the loss of attention due to the discomforts of pregnancy and then the arrival of the baby?*

   You don't have to feel left out, but you will have to adjust. So start now. Get your wife to include you in whatever she can—cravings, aches, pains, exhaustion, and excitement. If you do feel like you need her to be available and she can't, don't pout or be a martyr. Let her know how you feel and find a time you can share.

5. *Many men, particularly, first-time fathers, are very nervous around their pregnant wives.*
    You may be so afraid to touch your wife that you'll barely be able to kiss her goodnight. This is pretty common and very unnecessary. Let your wife know you're a little nervous about her tender condition. She can tell you if something you're doing is a problem or not.

6. *You may be very emotional right now.*
    Your wife may be the one going through the hormonal changes, but you may be feeling more emotional than usual too. As delighted as you may be, the thought of fatherhood may freak you out. You may feel panicked, overjoyed, needy, and loved all at the same time. Talk to your wife. She's certainly feeling the same thing.

7. *Do you have a clear vision of yourself as a father?*
    Think of how you see yourself and share it with your wife. Just talking about how your role will change will help you get used to the idea.

WHAT ELSE CAN WE DO?

If you can't sleep, have sex, and don't feel much like going out, what can you do together? Use this time to get closer to each other. On those nights you can't even think of moving, get some books, switch on the television, and just be together, holding hands. After the baby comes, these quiet moments will be few and far between. Which brings us to another helpful hint, the first trimester is the perfect time to begin planning your adjustment to the arrival of the baby. This is a great way to focus on things you have some control over, instead of those things you can just panic about.

Just as a good marriage doesn't come without a lot of hard work and planning, being good parents means doing your homework, too. You must both be prepared for what will happen in about eight months. Now, some people are very superstitious and won't plan a thing until they've made it to the second trimester. This is really a personal choice, but honestly, talking about the color you're going to paint the baby's room in the first trimester isn't going to jinx your pregnancy.

QUIET TIMES

For all our recommendations to talk, to be open, and to be honest, there will also be times when that's the last thing in the world you want to do or be. You may feel that you're talked out, that you have nothing to say to each other. Don't worry, this too is normal and will pass. Try to maintain a social life, if you have the strength, but avoid those situations that can be emotionally loaded. It's really too early to confront the problems your extended families may create for you. Save these conflicts for a time when you're not so emotionally drained. Try to stay as positive as possible.

BE REAL

It's not uncommon for couples, particularly first-time parents, to have some very unrealistic expectations about how pregnancy is going to make them different or maybe better people. This isn't true, and it's not a good idea to put these unrealistic expectations on each other. If before you were pregnant, your husband used to spend an hour alone after work depressurizing, don't suddenly expect that your pregnancy will cause him to act differently. Nor will your wife necessarily become more maternal or more domestic than she was before. Remember, you need not and cannot depend on each other to meet all of your interpersonal needs. That's what friends are for.

MISCARRIAGE

The threat of miscarriage is a major preoccupation for many couples during the first trimester. Most miscarriages do occur during the first trimester, so this is not a misplaced anxiety. If you are having any indications that your pregnancy is at risk, it's impossible not to worry.

THE BEST ANYONE CAN SAY ABOUT A BAD EXPERIENCE

A miscarriage can occur for any number of reasons. They are quite common, particularly for first pregnancies or older women. Estimates are that at least 30 percent of all pregnancies end in miscarriage. They are rarely or never the fault of the mother-to-be, and they are not indicative of future problems.

Miscarriages happen for reasons that often cannot be explained. Most occur because the pregnancy is not a healthy one and should not run its course. Unless your miscarriage was an extraordinary one, your doctor will probably recommend that you wait for two or three months and then start again. Usually the second attempt works better than the first.

Despite all this rationalizing, a miscarriage is an emotional and violent experience not easily forgotten or understood. It has a tendency to confirm all our worst fears about our fitness to be a parent and sends most women into a depression punctuated by periods of self-blame and anger.

The weeks and months after a miscarriage can be very difficult for you and your relationship. You will suffer. You will mourn the loss of your unborn child in the same way you would the death of a living person, and you will have to spring back from the emotional and physical shock. Remember, you are not alone in your pain.

Just as you will feel like a total failure because you weren't able to do what everybody else does with such apparent ease, so will your husband. Once again, most of the sympathy will be directed at the woman, and the man may be left angry and alone. He has suffered a loss, too. He had a tremendous amount of emotion and ego invested in this baby and may also be suffering with worry that he is unfit to bring a healthy child into the world.

Unfortunately, this type of pain may isolate you, rather than bring you closer together. You must struggle through the urge to run and hide. Instead express your anger, your pain, your love for each other, and allow yourselves to grieve appropriately. With time, love, and usually the reassurance of reality, you will be able to get beyond this painful experience and return to a normally healthy sexy life, committed to conceive again.

If you are an emotionally healthy couple who agree on wanting a child for positive reasons, you will have one, one way or another.

FINAL EXAM

You're now really beginning a whole new way of life together. So, why not start on the right foot. Take a minute to honestly ask yourselves the following questions. This may help you overcome some of the emotional and physical upheaval of the first trimester and strengthen your relationship.

1. Are you telling your spouse what worries you?

2. Are you both comfortable with the obstetrician, plans for delivery, and the hospital?

3. Are you both clear on your financial situation?

4. Are you taking the time to say *I love you*?

5. Are you blaming your morning, afternoon, or evening sickness on your spouse?

6. Are you comfortable with the way your spouse is dealing with the pregnancy? Taking care of him or herself?

7. Are you both proud of what you've done? Are you telling each other?

8. Are you planning the future—the baby's room, whether you'll need to move, and how you'll squeeze in some time for yourselves?

9. Are you still acting like husband and wife, or are you acting like mommy and daddy?

10. Are you there for each other?

11. Are you both feeling good about your marriage? Are you sharing your positive feelings and finding gentle ways to discuss what you'd like to change?

THE SECOND TRIMESTER

There's no way to hide it anymore. Your stomach is now your most prominent feature. No baggy sweater is big enough to conceal it. You are well and truly pregnant. Now that your pregnancy is public information, your boss will have to be told about your plans, your career plans will need to be reconsidered, your living arrangements may need to change, and you will have to cope with new emotional upheavals and fears about your developing baby. Little by little your role is going to change. People will start to treat you as an expectant mother, and that's both a joyful and annoying experience.

I FEEL LIKE A NEW PERSON

The physical miseries of the first trimester have now passed, and many women feel better than they have ever felt in their lives. A better hormone balance and the excitement over the arrival of a child, minus the bulk of the third trimester, may help to contribute to your all-consuming sense of well-being. For many women, in fact. the second trimester is also a time of heightened sexuality. Your energy is back, your sex drive returns, and happily, you are not too large for sex to be comfortable. Since you can't possibly get pregnant again, you have nothing to fear and so much to look forward to, so enjoy. Show each other your love. Many couples say that they enjoyed some of the best sex of their lives together during the fourth, fifth, and sixth month of pregnancy.

WHOSE BODY IS THIS ANYWAY?

Probably the most significant adjustment you will have to make is to the major change in your physical appearance—your swelling belly. While your tummy is marvelous physical evidence that you are truly a mother-to-be, this changing body and your new image presents the biggest challenge to a husband and wife.

In a world telling us skinny, boyish bodies are better, it is very difficult for a woman to adjust to a rounder, obvious female, far-from-virginal body type. The first problem, therefore, for most couples is accepting this new you as sexy and attractive. You really have to learn to accept a new concept of physical beauty and sexuality.

Your second problem presents itself when you fully realize that you will soon carry the mantle of parent in addition to spouse and lover. Suddenly you're all grown up and so is your husband. Suddenly your worst feelings about parents—anybody's parents, but your own in particular, begin to worry you. Suddenly your husband is daddy, you're mommy, and he may feel that he is no longer married to a sexy young girl, but to a woman and mother. And, you now may see your husband as a grown-up man and father. How this change affects the two of you depends on many issues:

1. Your feelings about being responsible for another person.

2. What being an "adult" means to you.

3. Your feelings about getting older.

4. Being able to recognize and liberate the child in you so that you can still have fun.

5. Your feelings about your parents—those unresolved issues between a man and his mother and a woman and her father—and guarding against the negative transference of those feelings onto your spouse.

6. Your ability to build your identity without unconsciously aligning with your same-sex parent.

7. Your parents' reaction to your new status.

Now that you're pregnant, your father may no longer want to relate to you as his little girl. He may now treat you as a woman who belongs to another man. Your husband's mother may now see you as the competitor. On the positive side, most parents view their expectant children with a new respect, often accepting them as equals for the first time. However, whatever unresolved issues exist between you and your parents may now reemerge or intensify and will require resolution—directly through intervention and compromise or passively through acceptance. Don't let them disturb your union as a couple.

PUBLIC NOTICE

Now that you look pregnant, the world will respond to you as a pregnant woman and an object of unsolicited public attention. It's amazing. The way people will stare at you, you might believe they've never seen a pregnant woman before. Mind you, none of this staring ever leads to a seat on the bus or train. Short of sticking your tongue out, there isn't much you can do to stop the looks. Be proud of your blossoming belly. Ignore the gawking looks and try to remember that you are preserving the species and that your pregnancy is a very natural, healthy human function.

ELLA: Walking past a construction site in the summer is never easy. I thought once I was pregnant I'd get a break. Wrong. They gawked and whistled with these stupid grins on their face. All I could think was these guys are sick.

EVERYBODY'S AN EXPERT

Perhaps worse than the staring, many people now feel compelled to give you unsolicited advice. While you're standing in the deli ordering a dozen bagels, some woman you've never seen before will begin telling you that onion bagels gave her terrible gas when she was pregnant and, she can tell you're having a girl because of the way you're carrying and, don't worry if you wanted a boy, you'll love your baby no matter what and on and on.

The body of a pregnant woman suddenly is an open topic of concern and discussion for any stranger who has an opinion. Most of these people will fall into the category of minor or major annoyances, but some can be quite negative and frightening. This is the last thing you need right now. So, what can you do?

Verbalizing your anger at these people will only lead to an aggravating and exhausting argument. The best thing you can do is disengage yourself from the conversation. If the remarks being made are not brief, and a polite "thank you" doesn't put an end to the conversation, interrupt, say "thank you" again, and turn your head the other way. Just turn the person off. Stop listening and move away.

SO MANY MEN, SO LITTLE TIME

Many obviously pregnant women find more men whistle at them on the street and make passes at them then before they were pregnant. Even if they were slim and gorgeous.

> *MARYANNE: There was this really handsome guy at my office. All the single women were nuts for him. We'd met a few times, but I'd hardly say we were friends. In my fourth month, he starts dropping by to say hello every afternoon. Big smiles. Long chats.*

When Maryanne asked her colleague why he was suddenly so interested in her, he unabashedly admitted that he loved pregnant women. This is very common. Many men are very turned on by a woman carrying a child. Why? Well, you are obviously sexually active, and you're also both voluptuous and comfy. Fortunately, for Maryanne, her husband felt the same way. Unfortunately, many women are not that lucky. Betsy and Stu, for example, faced the biggest crisis of their marriage once her belly started to show.

TURN OFF

STU: Betsy kept telling me how much she loved me. I knew she wanted to hear the same from me. All I could say was, "I know you do, honey." I was horrified by my actions. But this large woman . . . I didn't love her. I loved Betsy. The Betsy who's small and thin, built like a dancer. This didn't look like that Betsy.

Stu truly wanted this child as much as Betsy, and whenever he could forget about this new rounder Betsy he could remember how deeply he loved his wife. It was all very confusing. "Pregnant women never bothered me before, so why was I so repelled by Betsy? I really did some major soul-searching." Stu kept looking at their wedding and honeymoon pictures, trying to remember that the pregnant Betsy was this very same woman. It really didn't help though. Stu knew that even if this was his Betsy, it was the Betsy in the pictures that he loved and not this fat woman.

Luckily, Stu was honest enough to recognize and admit they had a serious problem and needed to get help. At his suggestion, he and Betsy decided to talk to a counselor. After some painful self-exploration, Stu realized that his problem wasn't really with Betsy, but with his memories of his own overweight childhood. An obese child, he had suffered years of jeering about his size. Though he finally lost his weight, he never forgot that pain. He lived in fear that he would have a fat wife and fat children.

At first, Stu's revelations only made Betsy feel even worse. She also valued a slim figure and felt the same way Stud did. She didn't want to be fat. She had struggled to stay thin herself, but she also understood that her new larger size was part of being pregnant and only a temporary condition.

How did Stu and Betsy resolve their problem? The two most important factors were time—the greatest healer of them all—and understanding. They both came to accept that Betsy's condition and body shape was not permanent. Stu accepted that his feelings were unusual and that they were his problem. He did his best not to make Betsy feel bad and tried not to be critical of her. He constantly reminded himself that her body hadn't changed because she was sloppy or self-indulgent, and he was thereby able to strike an uneasy peace between his fears and the physical realities of pregnancy. He never did grow completely comfortable with Betsy having a belly, and for the duration of the pregnancy was only able to have sex on rare occasions.

> BETSY: *I'm not going to say it didn't hurt. But I did understand Stu's problem. And that helped me to remember there was nothing wrong with me. It's always best to have the most important person in your life feel good about you, but this time it didn't happen. I got a lot of very positive support from the men and women in my office. Our parents were also very supportive and Stu really did the best he could.*

Had they never investigated the source of the bad feelings growing between them, Betsy may soon have been consumed by hurt and anger at Stu. In addition to his other miseries, Stu would then be left feeling guilty and ultimately angry at Betsy. Once this dynamic was established between them, their relationship probably would have degenerated to the point of being irreparable. But because they were able to communicate, that didn't happen. Stu was never able to change his feelings, but because they both understood and accepted the source of the problem, they got past it. Keeping in mind that it was only a matter of time before the baby was born, they knew that everything would be fine again.

TIME HEALS

This illustrates a very important point. Almost all of the problems you may encounter during your pregnancy pass with time—if they are handled in an intelligent and amicable manner. Since you are dealing with a precise amount of time, you can always remember that the end will come. You will feel healthy, slim, and sexy again.

I'M SORRY I'M PREGNANT?

Now that your pregnancy is no longer a secret, you will have to deal with other people's feelings about your condition. Most people will express great pleasure and excitement about the coming blessed event, but you will also encounter some jealousy and resentment.

Janice and her friend Pat had started trying to conceive at the same time. They were good friends and shared everything, including doctor's advise and fertility tips. After only three months, however, Pat was pregnant. Janice wasn't.

> *PAT: Janice and I joked that she'd be pregnant any day. She was very optimistic and supportive, but when I was in my sixth month and nothing had happened for her, I had to stop seeing her. She got really petty, jealous. I couldn't be unhappy about anything. I couldn't talk about my pregnancy, good or bad. I had to stop seeing her. It just wasn't fair.*

This does unfortunately happen to many friends. And, honestly, the best thing you can do is to keep away from the jealous person. You can offer encouragement and support, but when that is no longer accepted good-naturedly, it's time to bow out politely. You shouldn't have to sacrifice your own good feelings or bear the burden of your friend's frustration.

WHAT ARE YOU, NUTS?

Don't be surprised. You will hear it. From single friends, friends who don't want children, your parents, co-workers—basically, anyone who has had a negative parenting experience, anyone who is afraid of the change that will occur in their relationship with you, or anyone who can't deal with growing up.

PIA: Ben was having his own problems with the idea of being a father. We'd always been so footloose. His buddies kept ribbing him about how a baby would cramp his style. I could see it in his eyes. Panic, anger, confusion. Finally, we talked. Then he talked to his buddies. Told them they would either respect his decision, help him through the transition, or buzz off. I'm glad they all stuck with him.

TAKING CARE OF BUSINESS

Now's the time to deal with the issue of what you're going to do about your job, checking on benefits and deciding how long you're going to be out or if you are coming back at all.

Be prepared for tons of congratulations and a little sexist backlash. While many of your co-workers will take your pregnancy in stride, you may find others have some very vocal and sexist ideas about pregnant women.

Beverly was a highly valued executive at the agency at which she worked and never expected anyone would question her performance because she was pregnant.

BEVERLY: We're in this meeting and the discussion is getting hot. I took the hard line on a couple of pressing issues. I knew my position was based on good business sense, not hormones. Well, this very senior guy quips, "Don't mind, Bev, she's pregnant." How do you deal with that? Suddenly everybody's smiling at you like you're a child, and they're certainly not taking you seriously.

There is no tried and true method for how to neutralize sexist remarks other than to behave professionally even in the face of total stupidity. Today, most people are horrified by this sort of bad behavior and will ignore it. Rise above it at the moment it happens, but you may want to take it up privately later.

C'EST LA VIE

Just as you may want to be taken seriously on the job, your focus in the second trimester does start to shift from your job to your baby and home life. Filled with a wonderful sense of well-being and anticipation, your interest and involvement in anything other than your pregnancy may whither. Some of the nagging problems you face every day may suddenly seem unimportant. Your body is preparing another life to enter into the world. This is a deep and primal experience. You are part of the human evolutionary chain—the millions of women that have given birth before you and will after you. Your awareness of this greater role in life has a definite impact on your motivation. It may be hard for you to get that management report out on time. You're not lazy. You're involved in something more important. You're preparing for the arrival of your child, and you will be very preoccupied with some of the deepest feelings any person can ever expect to feel in this life.

I'M NOT YOUR MOTHER

While a man's inability to become sexually aroused by a pregnant wife will pass once the pregnancy is over, the feeling that his beloved wife is now a mother will not pass. If this realization does not generate positive feelings, it will totally disrupt your relationship long after the baby arrives.

Many men do go through a period of seeing their wife as mother. For most, this passes, but in some cases it develops into a marriage-threatening situation. The problem usually manifests itself in several different ways. One is the Madonna complex. This is an unconscious re-creation of what a man believes was the significant, original birth of mankind. No matter what his wife might have been before she became the mother of his child, and no matter how sexually active they were, she is now a mother, and there-fore virginal and innocent. Like his mother, who he idolizes and adores, his wife now deserves a special place of honor—on a pedestal right next to the Virgin Mary. In this position, there is no way she can be a real person, never mind an object of sexual desire.

At the opposite extreme is the man who dislikes or resents and is angry at his mother. This man may have suf-fered under a controlling, dominating, and suffocating mother. The ambivalent or hostile feelings he still carries from his childhood he now unconsciously transfers to his wife. Since she is now a mother, she is, therefore, someone he is very angry with. His lover has been transformed into a powerful person, a mother. And to him this means someone who can now dominate and overpower him. Now that his wife is more powerful than he is, he is, of course, intimidated and afraid of her. It follows that out of his fear he will seek to avoid intimacy with his wife.

The third man for whom *wife* becomes *mother* is the man who neither worships nor hates his mother. Actually, he may be very fond of his mother, but he has never associated his mother with sex. Most likely he grew up in a home where his mother was not a sexual person, and his father didn't respond to her in that way. His parents were probably a very typical couple about whom their children say, "I can't imagine them ever having sex, but they had to do it a least once because I'm here." This man as he begins to see his baby growing inside his wife's belly, may lose his ability to envision her as a sexual person, no matter how loudly she protests.

Larry and Roberta became very acutely aware of their problem in the sixth month of Roberta's pregnancy.

ROBERTA: Every time Larry and I attempted to have sex, he would lose his erection. He was certainly turned on and interested in wanting to please me. It didn't make any sense, and it was getting very frustrating. I couldn't get angry with him. He was as perplexed as I was. We decided to get professional help.

LARRY: It took a few very intense, and a little embarrassing, therapy sessions to realize I was suffering from two fairly common male fears. Now that Roberta was pregnant, she was a mother, like my mother, and I was really confused. My mother hadn't been a sexual person, so neither could Rober-

ta. Besides that, I was worried that sex would hurt the baby. No matter what the obstetrician said I could not believe that sex was okay.

After listening to Roberta in the joint sessions, pounding her chest insisting she wasn't his mother, Larry finally believed that she was the old, sexually active woman he had married. Solving the second problem took a little more time and was alleviated through a common sex therapy practice. Roberta and Larry continued to engage in affectionate sex play, starting with hugs, cuddles, kisses, and then building until the day came when Larry was able to let instinct and emotion take the place of thinking and fear. He was able to enjoy intercourse with Roberta, and the fact that she was happier afterwards, convinced him that everything was okay.

IS THE BABY OKAY?

Your first trimester anxieties about miscarriage may be well behind you, but now your anxieties shift from your fear of losing the baby to your fears that the baby won't be healthy.

Many women find themselves troubled by nightmares of giving birth to a very sick child. They look for proof that everything is okay, say silent prayers to plead for a healthy baby. Any unexpected pain, feeling or lack of feeling takes on tremendous importance and can create a terrible panic.

MARLENE: Toward the end of my sixth month I started spotting. I freaked. This was my first baby and I knew first pregnancies can be rough. I got in bed and called the doctor. He told me to stay in bed until the bleeding stopped. It ended in about an hour. I went in for a checkup the next day.

Everything was fine. The doctor told me that sometimes these things happen. Pregnancy doesn't always go by the rules. He had to do a lot of explaining to convince me my baby was going to be okay. It did finally sink in.

Marlene did have some physical reason to get nervous, but it doesn't take anything more than a bad dream or a nagging fear to get you nervous. This is another time two brains are better than one. Rely on each other to soothe your anxieties and get a grip on reality. Remember, the spouse who isn't frightened at this particular moment must step in and diffuse the anxiety. Don't belittle your spouse's fears because they seem illogical; logic has nothing to do with it, so just help to rebuild a sense of security.

AMNIOCENTESIS

During the second trimester you must decide for or against amniocentesis. Amniocentesis is a fairly accurate screening for some forms of birth defects, particularly Down Syndrome. It is a powerful diagnostic tool and also a helpful way to relieve some of your anxiety about the well-being of your baby. Most doctors recommend any woman over age 35 have the test.

We all hear ugly rumors about the horrors of medical practice, and amniocentesis is one medical procedure that brings with it much rumor and speculation. The test does, in fact, carry a very small risk of fetal injury, and this should be evaluated. If you and your husband know that under no circumstances would you consider aborting your pregnancy, then there is absolutely no reason for you to consider going through this ordeal. On the other hand, if you do decide in favor of having the test, just making that decision and anticipating the results is both a relief and a continuing anxiety. Once you do learn that everything is fine, however, you will feel a tremendous sense of relief.

Tommy and Mary felt the best way to face amniocentesis was to go through the test together. Mary was pretty comfortable. At 38 years of age, she felt the test was an unquestioned necessity. Tommy, however, was a nervous wreck.

MARY: I was lying on the table, Tommy was holding my hand. The doctor came out with the needle and Tommy passed out cold. Everybody spent so much time reviving Tommy that the test seemed like nothing.

While this is one way of defusing anxiety, it's not the recommended approach. If one or both of you is very nervous about the test, get a full and accurate medical description of the procedure and possible side effects long before you undergo the procedure. Understanding and mutual support is really the best way to combat uncertainty.

Fortunately, most babies are healthy, and you will never have to face the painful decision of whether to abort or not to abort a fetus. You should, however, advise your doctor to what extremes you will go to preserve the life of a damaged child. It's important that he understand what you feel and be prepared to deal with whatever emergency procedures may be necessary at the time of delivery. This is an extremely personal and frightening issue to face. Both you and your spouse must discuss it openly and reach an agreement that you can act on and live with long before you are caught up in the heat of labor.

BOY OR GIRL?

Another result of amniocentesis is that you will know the sex of your child. Sometimes you can determine whether it will be a boy or a girl by just looking at the sonogram screen. Decide whether or not you want to know the sex before you have the test. If one of you wants to know and the other doesn't, that's fine, but agree on a way to handle it, and be sure to advise your doctor of your decision. And, most important, respect each other's feelings.

NO COMPARISONS

LAURA: I didn't know what got into him. Peter came rushing into the house, grabbed me by the hand, and said, "Laura, hurry up, go lie down in bed." Then he rushed in, put his ear on my belly, and started patting my stomach. Suddenly he stopped. He had this panic-stricken expression and wouldn't tell me what was wrong. Finally he told me that a colleague's wife was due at the same time that I was. Well, this guy had felt his baby kick the night before. Peter couldn't feel our baby kick. He was convinced something was wrong.

Just as all children do not develop at the same pace, neither do all fetuses. Some fetuses are active and start kicking early in the fifth month. Others, lazy or calm, don't start kicking until well into the sixth month. To some extent, fetal activity is also affected by the mother's level of tension and how this is physiologically communicated to the developing baby. Remember, no two pregnancies are the same for either the mother-to-be or the fetus. Just because things aren't moving at the same pace as your friend's pregnancy doesn't mean that you have anything to worry about.

Also, some couples really get caught up in competing for the perfect pregnancy, the weirdest pregnancy, the toughest pregnancy. Don't spoil your experience by involving yourselves in this sort of behavior. It can really take all the pleasure out of your experience and create more tension than you need.

TO SHOP OR NOT TO SHOP

Now that you've got this new shape, what are you going to wear? You can't spend six months in sweat pants, particularly if you work, but you should try to keep wardrobe needs in perspective and reach an agreement on just how much you're going to spend. It's important to feel good about yourself, but do you really want to pay a lot of money for expensive clothes you may never wear again. It's a good idea to have a wardrobe budget that you both agree to—and stick to. Arguing over extravagances is not going to make either one of you happy right now. Once the child arrives, you may very well have to adjust to living under a tighter budget, so it's best to start off on the right foot.

LIVING QUARTERS

When is the right time to begin fixing up the baby's room? How much are you going to spend on furnishings? Superstition takes its toll here, and you may find you and your husband have very differing opinions. Try to strike a compromise. Most people do wait until the last trimester, some until after the delivery, but keep in mind it's important to not leave everything to the last minute. The baby's room should be ready when you come home from the hospital. Planning makes things easier, and once again, agree on a budget. It's very easy to get caught up in the moment and spend more than you can afford. You know how you usually work, so build a schedule that allows you to finish without too much last-minute pressure.

SIBLING RIVALRY

Now that your pregnancy is obvious, your other children will have lots of questions and need plenty of extra support. The arrival of a new brother or sister should not only be discussed with them, but they should also be included in the planning for the arrival. Most children will need a lot of help in understanding what it means to have a new baby in the family. The younger the children, obviously, the more help they will need. A child under two, for example, will not really be able to understand the change until the baby is home. At that point, they may then experience considerable jealousy when their new sibling seems to be the focus of all the attention and interest.

The older your children, the easier it will be for them to accept another child in the family. No matter what the age of your children, you must discuss your pregnancy with them. They should not be excluded from the arrival of their sibling, and they must be reassured that a new baby will not take your love away from them.

Try to point out how the arrival of the new baby will be valuable and helpful to the whole family. It is important to help your older child understand that the new baby will make everyone's life different and more meaningful. So often, young children like to be told the new baby will make them more grown up and that as the big brother or sister they will play an important part in the care of the new baby.

This is a nice feeling. It helps the older children to willingly give of themselves without suffering over the attention lavished on the infant.

It is also important to make sure that this new birth does not become the dominant theme of your family. There are other important events taking place in all of your lives. The truth is that these months are far more critical to the psychological well-being of your other children then they are to the developing child. By all means follow your doctor's orders and take no unnecessary risks, but don't become so obsessed with what's going on internally that you exclude the other people who need you now.

The same is true with regard to your relationship with your spouse. Do not forget to take the needs of your spouse seriously. Before you became pregnant you both had individual needs and problems. Just because you're pregnant, your spouse's needs should not become secondary to your condition. If your spouse needs to talk to you about his life, never communicate an attitude of indifference to what he has to say, that his feelings can't possibly be as important as your pregnancy. That's not the way to keep a relationship together. You should, for this reason, always remember that a family means the two of you, plus a baby. All three of you are creating a new life together.

BACK TO BASICS

You should never lose track of the fact that three does not replace two. The husband and wife being alone with each other is another aspect, actually the heart, of the family unit. It is the original unit and an entity that should always remain and have a life of its own. The family trio, quartet, or even quintet has its own life. The individual relationships that exist between mother and child, and father and child, and mother and father, should also have their own unique essence and be nurtured and cultivated. Human beings require attention and positive nurturing to grow and thrive at any age—adult or child. Every individual in the family requires individual attention. Before the new arrival, before things snowball into chaos, you and your spouse should develop a plan to insure no one is abandoned during the change. Set aside time to spend alone with your husband, for each of you to spend time alone with each child. Even if you spend just fifteen minutes a day alone with each child and your husband, it will go a long way toward elimination of hurt feelings.

FEELING MORE DEPENDENT

As your body blossoms into advanced pregnancy, you will certainly begin to feel that your wonder-woman days are behind you. Now, pregnancy doesn't make you a wimp, but it may arrest some of your physical capabilities or you may feel frightened to do some of the things you did before.

You won't be hoisting furniture around the house or lugging anything heavy for that matter. Climbing a ladder to do something as usual as changing a lightbulb may make you feel uneasy. Taking a two-mile run may cause a funny pulling feeling or you may want to shield your belly from strangers on the street. If you are having a difficult pregnancy, your doctor may prescribe total bed rest, and you will, undoubtedly, find yourself asking your spouse to help do things you would normally do yourself.

Just as some women find the adjustment to this more dependent position easier than others, so some husbands respond better to being on call than others. If your husband is a bit lazy or if you normally take care of him, this can be a difficult readjustment. But it's a good thing you're learning the worst about him now. After the baby is born, he'll have to carry even more weight. This early warning gives you plenty of time to work things out.

Don't whine, bitch, or play the martyr. And most important, don't act like a helpless little girl or his mother. Work this through as two adults. Tell your husband this is one of the most important ways he can be involved in your pregnancy. After all, it is. He's taking care of you and, therefore, taking care of his unborn child.

WOMEN ARE AFTER MY HUSBAND

Women are not supposed to be our enemies, but this isn't a perfect world. There are women who really love husbands, particularly pregnant husbands. And there are husbands who have always been looking for the perfect excuse to have an affair.

If your husband is being cornered by vipers, you can help him. But if he's flirting his way through your pregnancy, letting you know how turned off he is by your body, you have problems. Get help. And face facts. Things aren't going to get better when you approach the point in your pregnancy when sex is out of the question.

BRINGING IT ALL BACK HOME

You would have to be a saint or a total fool not to be disturbed by some of the things that will happen to you now that your pregnancy is public. But, remember, neither one of you is to blame for what the world is doing. Instead of fighting, find a solution, unite, and talk about the pressures. If you establish a comfortable home environment, you will have just the right situation in which to defuse some of the grief and get some support. Once again, these outside pressures are likely to increase after birth. Work out the kinks now, and you'll be in much better shape later.

FINAL EXAM

1. Are you both comfortable with how the pregnancy is progressing?

2. What unresolved issues still exist between the two of you?

3. Do you have a better picture of what the future will bring?

4. Are you comfortable with your doctor? Have you discussed all of your medical preferences and set the ground rules for your treatment?

5. Are you helping to ease each other's anxieties about the health of the baby?

6. Are you forcing each other into new and uncomfortable parent roles?

7. Do you feel alone or are you going through this pregnancy together?

8. How are you both feeling about your friends? Your parents?

9. Are you talking about parental interference, your feelings about your parents, their relationship, and what you do and don't want to carry over into your family relationship?

10. Are you looking at your spouses honestly or are you wrongly blaming them for your own confusion?

11. Have you openly confronted your attitudes to discipline and parenting?

12. Have you developed a way to reconcile your differences?

13. Have you talked about money, started to work out a budget?

14. Are you consoling, comforting, and rewarding each other as you take the first step toward parenthood?

THE LAST TRIMESTER

Now you're really pregnant. There's no escaping it. In approximately twelve weeks you're going to bring a living, breathing child into the world. And there isn't a minute of your last trimester that you're not reminded of this. For possibly the first time in your pregnancy you can really feel life growing inside of you. There is an evident heartbeat, movement, kicking—sometimes so strong that you think you can see it—and the ever more cumbersome burden of your belly.

Women differ in their reactions to this change in their bodies. Some women welcome the opportunity to relax about their weight and maintaining their figure. They enjoy the adventure of shopping for maternity clothes and even feel they can use their pregnancy to take a break from all their tailored business suits and add a few ruffles or vice versa.

I FEEL PRETTY, I THINK?

Even at this advanced stage of pregnancy, a woman is still sexy to many people. The woman who feels just as good and positive about herself will find the last three months of her pregnancy the most joyful time. Free of many of the fears of the early months of her pregnancy, she can relax and enjoy the positive attention from those who are anxious to share the experience and excitement with her.

Sexy, though you may be to some people, however, it might be hard to remember this when you can't bend over and tie your shoelaces. Even if you have kept to a healthy diet and continued to exercise (most doctors do recommend sensible exercise throughout a pregnancy), you are going to be large and uncomfortable. If you have gained far too much weight or are carrying in a peculiar way, the burden may be even greater.

While most women just accept their shape as a temporary thing, many do begin to worry that they will never regain their sexy shape and will be bulky and pear-shaped forever. Some women, in fact, become unnecessarily sensitive about their bodies and feel repulsed by themselves. They often project these negative feelings onto their husbands, rationalizing that they have no interest in affection or sex because their husband is no longer attracted to them. This is a self-perpetuating problem. If you don't like yourself, don't feel comfortable with yourself, your husband will pick this up, and he will also pick up your unspoken aversion to him. When Marsha confronted her husband about her feeling that he was no longer attracted to her, it was made clear that she was the one avoiding sexual play with her husband.

I guess it started in the seventh month. I used to love getting undressed in front of Bill. It was such an intimate . . . sexy thing, even if we just went right to sleep. Once I had this big belly I started coming to bed dressed, covered up. I didn't want him near me, never mind looking at me. I felt deformed.

Bill, who was anxiously looking forward to the baby, was not turned off by Marsha. He accepted that they could no longer have intercourse and was perfectly content with cuddling and hugging. He loved to look at Marsha's full body and was more desirous than ever for intimate contact.

IS MY WIFE IN THERE?

As your pregnancy begins to restrict your physical, social, and sexual activity, the role between partners begins to change, and like any change this creates stress. As your stamina lessens and movement becomes more difficult, your husband may begin to feel that you are less available to him. He may, in fact, feel that he's been abandoned in favor of the baby.

> *Suzanne was totally exhausted at the end of her day. I knew she wanted to continue to work. It helped to keep her mind off the pregnancy, and let's face it, the money was nice. I understood that, but I resented it, too. When she came home from work, all she wanted to do was to have supper and go to bed. It wasn't just the sex that I missed. Suzanne is my best friend. I really missed the talks, the socializing, the doing-nothing time that we used to share.*

There's no doubt that you need your sleep now, but you don't have to sulk off to the bedroom the minute you get home, closing people out and acting like a cranky adolescent. Try to schedule your evenings so there is time for a nap and for your husband. Maybe you could leave work a half hour earlier and get a short nap in before your husband is home. Easy for us to say, right? What about those nights you can hardly drag yourself in the door? Invite your husband to share your nap, or at least to come to bed and read while you snooze. Lie close together, rub your belly, and feel your new baby.

What about food? Well, there's always take-out, there are always frozen dinners, and you might try some advance planning. On those days when you feel like you could climb Mt. Everest, take some time to prepare the week's meals in advance. Freeze them and heat them up when you're ready. This will help you to eat healthier and alleviate any feelings of guilt.

YOU DON'T LOVE ME ANYMORE

Many women, while they're at their roundest, are overwhelmed by a deep-seated concern that their husbands will no longer find them attractive, and that when they can no longer have intercourse, he will look and find other women more attractive.

Joan became obsessed with the fact that when she and her husband walked down the street he looked at all the pretty, slim young women. Now, he had always looked, but she had never been sensitive to it when she was slim and sexy. She was so uncomfortable and insecure that she just assumed he was behaving this way because he found her undesirable.

Now, this is a tough topic to talk about. You feel so vulnerable, and you'd have to be blind to believe that you currently look better than when you were a toned size ten. But you have to bring your feelings out in the open. At this stage of your pregnancy feelings are often intensified, and it's all too easy to get into a frenzy over the simplest misunderstanding. It's very likely that your husband feels just as you do. He will be just as delighted as you to have a healthy baby and a slim, sexy wife again, but that doesn't mean he's looking to jump on every woman that walks by.

> *It was amazing. Out of nowhere I would find myself scream-ing, "You don't care about me, you don't care about the baby, you don't care about anything, do you?" But I have to admit Steve handled me beautifully. Of course, I found out later that he had been talking things over with his father who had seen his mother through seven children. So, I guess he had gotten a pretty good preview of what was coming.*

Something that may help to relieve some of this anxiety is to keep up an active intimate life. Maybe you can't have intercourse, but that doesn't mean that you can't hug, kiss, cuddle, or relieve each other's sexual needs in other ways. Be silly about your protruding stomach. Talk to it. Laugh about it. Talk about the exercise program you're both going to get involved in after the baby comes. Remind each other of how much you share together and how much closer the baby will bring you.

Well, in a perfect world, all husbands would be turned on by their wives' big bellies, but as we mentioned in earlier chapters, this isn't always the case. Hard though it may be to hear the words that he finds you awful to look at, it's bet-ter that you hear them now. They are usually the reflection of a bigger problem your husband has about motherhood and parenting. Once you know what's going on, you can both move to resolve the problem before it creeps into your marriage and becomes a negative influence.

PLAN AHEAD

Now is the time for all well-prepared couples to plan for the delivery of their child. This is something you should tackle as a twosome. Planning is good medicine. It helps you to regain a sense of control and it gives you something into which you can channel all your anxieties about labor and the health of the baby. It gives you a slew of things to share with your husband, including, if you have not already done this, planning and hiring some household help and organizing work schedules. After all, the plans that you are making include both of you and reflect both your needs.

Of course, your prelabor plans should include updating your doctor on how much pain you're willing to tolerate during labor and when you'll go for some anesthesia. Even though you're planning on natural childbirth, the pain may become too great. You may feel very strident in your belief that natural childbirth is the more womanly thing to do, that it makes you less of a mother to have help. But most women do have help, particularly if they have an extended delivery.

BACK TO SCHOOL

Today, more than ever, there are more social and psychological aids available to expectant couples than at any other time, and you should definitely take advantage of these programs. Even if you are not going to have a natural delivery, there is tremendous value to participating in natural childbirth training programs. You will both be trained in breathing techniques and exercises to do together at home. And, if nothing else, you will both benefit from the laughter and fun they can lead to. Laughter is a great way to reduce stress, and doing the exercises together really helps to establish the sense that you are both having a baby.

It took Arlene and Bill several evenings to perfect one of the exercises.

You know the one. The woman sits in bed with her knees bent, leaning into her husband's legs. Sounds easy, right? Bill and I were like human pretzels. He practically had his feet in my mouth. By the time we finished laughing, we both felt much more relaxed about our ability to handle what was coming up.

These classes provide a real opportunity to share with each other and with the other couples who are your classmates. You can gain so much by discussing your anxieties, joys, and concerns with others going through the same experience. Your obstetrician will be able to direct you to childbirth classes. Most hospitals offer parenting classes and even organize groups for future parents.

SHOP TILL YOU DROP

For most couples, except for the superstitious, now is the time to shop for furniture, baby clothing, and to create a room or space for the new baby. Some couples, superstitious about planning in advance, prefer to have a relative or friend—or the father, himself—rush out and buy everything once the baby is born healthy.

Rob and Jackie had spent the entire eight months ignoring Jackie's pregnancy. Except for the monthly checkups, they acted as if nothing was really happening. Jackie had so many over-sized sweaters that she never really bought maternity clothes.

Most couples, however, do feel that they are missing out on a real bonding experience by not using this time to enjoy the planning and projection of the infant to come. The truth is that even if you do not plan and don't feel as though you've missed anything, you will be less prepared, not only in terms of a room and clothes, but also in your emotional readiness for a child.

The lesson to be learned from this is not to ignore reality as Jackie and Rob did, but to reach an agreement as to how you will deal with the pregnancy. The plan you both feel comfortable with is going to work best for you, no matter what anybody tells you.

AM I READY FOR THIS, OR WHAT?

Superstitious or not, during the last trimester most women do develop a pronounced nesting instinct and are bitten by the bug to get the house ready. Suddenly all the laundry must be done, all the kitchen cabinets must be cleaned out, the bathroom cabinets must be neat and tidy, all the clothes must be neatly organized in the closet. How much this affects your relationship is directly related to how obsessive you become, how willing your husband is to clean along with you, or how able he is to let you do your own thing.

> *I was due in about three days. Don't ask me what possessed us, but we decided to have a dinner party. Brian, me, and a few friends were sitting in front of the fireplace. They were all drinking brandy. I had my Perrier. Suddenly, I just stood up, went to the sun room, and came back in with the ironing board and the iron. I set it up, plugged it in, and proceeded to iron. Everybody just looked at me like I was nuts. I just told them not to pay any attention to my ironing. I just had to get it done because I wasn't sure when I would get a chance to do it again. The party went on, no problem.*

This desire to be ready is an important part of getting ready for the arrival of the baby. Many people go through it. Stella, for example, made sure that she'd had her hair cut and all the household paperwork in order at least a week before delivery. What motivates this need for perfect domestic and personal organization? Something that motivates most human behavior in times of stress: the underlying psychological need to feel a sense of control. And, this is not a behavior particular to women. It is just as common for the man to go out and buy footballs and soccer equipment, even though he knows the infant won't be using it for years. Fathers need to feel involved, too. They need to feel that they have some influence and some control over the changes that are about to occur in their lives. Of course, this sports equipment is no more helpful, or no more necessary at this moment, then his wife's ironing. The daddy-to-be simply needs to feel that he's doing something meaningful.

NOBODY NEEDS ME

Many men do begin to feel that they're not needed. This feeling often begins in the last trimester and can continue into the following first six months of the baby's life. It's important, therefore, to remember to include your husband. The childbirth classes are a good beginning. Shop together for maternity clothes, the baby's clothes, and furniture. Let hubby paint the room, let him buy sports equipment, let him plan anyway he wants to.

A lot of men don't understand that the reassurance and affection you are asking for from them is a very important contribution. They somehow don't appreciate how important this is to you now. You must, therefore, let your husband know how you feel about it. If he is already feeling as though he's lost his attractive, active wife, this misunderstanding will only make this time even more emotionally upsetting for him. Mind you, it's no barrel of laughs for the woman who senses that her husband feels this way, but feels helpless to change it.

WHAT KIND OF CREEP AM I?

Once again, you must discuss this. A man who has these feelings, yet knows that he loves his wife and is delighted to be having a baby, may experience a great deal of turmoil. He may feel guilty about finding other women attractive, and blame himself for having these feelings. The first thing he needs to know is that his feelings are natural. As long as a person is a sexual person, they will notice other attractive people.

It may, however, be very difficult for your husband to admit to these feelings. In fact, it may take some outside help to get him to open up to you. You may get help and support from the other couples in your childbirth classes. Just hearing that some of the other men in the group have survived the same problems can be very therapeutic. If you feel that you need more help, your group leader may be able to direct you to a good professional counselor.

Try to make it easier for your husband to open up. It will also be easier for him if he senses that you're comfortable with your pregnancy. If you feel insecure and he knows it, he'll obviously find it more difficult to talk. This may not be the most pleasant conversation you'll ever have, but it is a necessary one, and you should try to avoid a fight. It will help if the mother-to-be is getting a lot of support from other men—like her father or brother or male friends. They can reassure her that she really does look great and is desirable.

IF THIS IS SO NATURAL, WHY AM I SO NERVOUS?

Even for the most committed mothers-to-be, facing labor is an awesome experience. In fact, most women have heard enough old-wives' tales and horror stories to be more than a little anxious about labor. By this time, you will be torn between the desire to have the baby and be rid of your big, uncomfortable belly and the desire to postpone what might be a very painful ordeal. Roz, for example, when asked how she felt about her upcoming labor, simply answered, "I just want it to happen and be over already."

No one can really determine how long delivery will take. So, along with all your other planning, it may not be a bad idea to plan some activity for the labor period. Of course, just the word *labor* suggests that it is an arduous experience, so it makes perfect sense that you may develop some irrational fears. If you are going to deliver under anesthesia, you may suddenly develop fears of dying during delivery. This is one of the key reasons many women choose natural childbirth.

These fears have more to do with a sense that you have lost control than with any real physical or medical danger. Your obstetrician can quickly put most of your fears to rest. Death in childbirth, even under anesthesia, is extremely rare these days. But if you are afraid, discuss it with your doctor, and if it makes you feel more comfortable, talk to the anesthesiologist. It's a good idea to include your husband in these discussions.

Beth had never had a child. She was twenty-two and living with a couple who were expecting their second baby. During a conversation, her pregnant friend mentioned the episiotomy. Beth had never heard about this procedure and was upset and frightened by the thought of it. Four years later, when she became pregnant with her own child, she suddenly became fixated and terrified by the recollection of what her friend had told her and the pain it would cause her. Despite what friends had told her: "They do it during a contraction, you'll never feel it," the episiotomy became a real focus for all her anxieties about delivering her child.

The resolution of this fear, like most fears relating to pregnancy, is that this episiotomy, which is a very small incision made to ensure that the vaginal opening isn't torn when the baby passes, is no worse than any minor surgical cut. And, it's true you do not feel it. By the time the doctor makes this incision, you'll be so involved in your contractions that this will be the least of your concerns. Even during natural childbirth, your doctor will use local anesthesia or, at the very least, some topical novocaine to eliminate the pain.

We're not going to tell you that labor is fun. There is some discomfort. There is pain and in some cases it can be extreme. But there are also moments of incredible elation and joy. There is no experience that can compare to the birth of a child.

UNEMPLOYMENT, HERE I COME

The answer to the question of when a woman should stop work is the same as that governing what sexual practices to engage in. You should be guided by the physical and emotional needs you share, and as long as it's comfortable, you should continue doing what makes you happy. Many women quit work a month before their due date. This leaves plenty of time to plan and rest for when the baby comes. Delivery is a stressful experience, and if you go into it rested and relaxed, it generally goes much more easily.

On the other hand, if financial considerations dictate

you work up to the last minute, quitting early may leave you more stressed. You'll now have plenty of time to worry about how you're going to make ends meet. Again, the right choice here is the one that works best in your particular circumstances. Don't feel obliged to follow anybody else's rules.

Most women plan to return to work when their baby is six months old. This decision obviously depends upon the company rules and just how secure your job is. But keep in mind that it is healthier for you to take plenty of time to regain your strength after the delivery. No matter how many peasants can have babies and go right back to picking rice, the same doesn't seem to work for Western women. Labor is a fatiguing experience. You should carefully evaluate how to get the most time off to recuperate. Give yourself at least a month or more if possible to recover and to get to know your infant. In fact, if you push yourself to get up and go too soon, you may be debilitated for much longer than you would have if you had taken care of yourself.

EVERY CHILD SHOULD BE A SECOND CHILD

It's an old joke, but it's true. Just like the first time you do anything, a first pregnancy and delivery is much more stressful than a second. A first delivery is often more painful and a little longer than it is for a mother giving birth for the second time. Of course, no two pregnancies are ever the same, even for the same woman. So, it pays to approach each delivery with an open mind and give some thought as to what may occur during the procedure.

PREMATURE DELIVERY

As you near the end of your pregnancy, you may find

yourself taking every little twinge to be the onset of labor. Many women do experience a false labor well before they're due, and although the pain may seem quite intense for this false start, you will recognize the real thing when it happens. You should, however, contact your doctor at the onset of any pain. You may indeed be delivering prematurely or need medical attention to ensure that you carry the baby full term. If this is the case, the best place for you to be is in a major university hospital. Premature delivery is dangerous, but it is no longer as risky to mother and child as it once was. It does, however, add an additional level of stress to an already emotional experience and will require the mutual support of both spouses.

THE HOSPITAL STAY AND DELIVERY

You won't really need to look at the calendar to know you're due any day now. All you'll have to do is take a good look at your body. Your stomach will have dropped significantly, and you will feel that you're carrying the baby much lower than before. Your doctor will want to see you more frequently now. He will watch your cervix, measuring and noting your rate of dilation. He will advise you not to plan any long trips or do any strenuous labor. Basically, it's time to sit tight and wait.

THE BIG COUNTDOWN

About two weeks before your expected due date, both you and your husband will start anxiously watching for the first signs of labor. If this is your first baby, like many other first-time parents, you will probably worry that labor will begin and you won't know it. It's not uncommon to ex-

145

perience a false labor. You may find yourself ready to run to the hospital when all of a sudden your pain will subside. When the real thing happens, believe me, you will know it. There is no way, never mind the old-wives' tales you've heard, for a baby to be born without the mother even knowing she is in labor.

It's right about now that you really start to appreciate all that preplanning you've been up to. What you've learned in your childbirth classes will help you to deal with the approaching birth as a unified supportive, and informed team.

WE'RE READY FOR ANYTHING

By this time, a well-prepared couple will have a suitcase packed, will have made firm arrangements for getting the woman to the hospital, and will know what to do in case of an emergency.

There's no need to repack your suitcase every night. Everything you need is in there. The only person who should even consider opening the suitcase is the future father. He might want to tuck a little gift or a card inside. Just a little something that his wife can find after the delivery that says "I love you" or "thank you."

Always have a get-me-to-the-hospital contingency plan. Just in case the moment to go to the hospital comes when your husband is out to lunch or at a meeting and can't be reached. A neighbor or a friend should be on call to drive. Under no circumstances should you drive yourself. Don't even think about it.

If this is your first pregnancy, you will probably be in for a long haul. In addition to all your other planning, plan something to do with yourself while you wait for the worst of labor to begin. Do a crossword puzzle, play cards, or you could even start addressing the birth announcements. Anything that can occupy you and your husband is fine.

FALSE ALARM

The minute Susan felt her first labor pain, she called her husband and told him to come and drive her to the hospital immediately.

When I got to the emergency room, I called the obstetrician. When I told him my contractions were only one an hour, he told me to go home and wait a few hours until they were coming one every ten minutes. It was hours before that happened. We rented a couple of videotapes, ate popcorn. I'm glad I was comfortable and at home.

Anna, on the other hand, was admitted to the OB ward on her first arrival.

What a mistake. I had to lay in bed listening to the moans and groans of other women for at least eight hours. It was emotionally draining. By the time my labor was intense enough to move me into the delivery room, I felt like I'd already delivered quints.

Dorothy and Stan, who already had one child, went to the movies at the first sign of labor. Dorothy knew that she had at least ten hours to go and that sitting home was only going to make her crazy. Other couples go out for a nice dinner. Do something that will be distracting and entertaining, take the time to talk about what's happening and what's going to happen. Try not to focus too much on the pain before you have to. It will just make your labor even more exhausting.

If, on the other hand, your pains are coming very consistently, at short intervals, by all means sound the alarm. Call your husband. Call your doctor, and make your condition very clearly understood when you arrive in the emergency room. In the midst of all the activity going on there, it is very easy to be overlooked. This is not the time to be polite or quietly wait your turn. Get yourself heard and attended to.

TRAINING PAYS OFF

One of the advantages of all that prenatal training is that you will not have to face delivery alone. Your husband will be there with you in the labor room to be supportive, to help with your breathing, and, hopefully, to be caring and affectionate.

Even if your situation turns out like Rose's it will still feel better to have your husband with you.

We had taken all of the childbirth classes together. Larry was primed and ready for the big day. Then, when it was zero hour, Larry lost it. He got so nervous, he couldn't remember how to breathe, never mind keep track of what I was doing. We had to leave the car and take a taxi. I had to pay. In the labor room, Larry was so distressed that the nurses were giving him all the attention. They were wheeling me into the delivery room, but they were still worried about Larry. It was okay, though. He distracted me from my pains, and that's what all that training is about anyway.

I PLEAD THE FIFTH

A word about labor. It is not called *labor* for nothing, and it can provoke even the most demure, mild-mannered women to some rather extreme behavior. You are not responsible for, nor should you feel guilty about, whatever you say or do during these hours. Pain does strange things to people. After all, you are here to do another job, a tough one, and that is to deliver a baby. Of course, if you can be calm and positive despite the pain, it will be helpful and maybe easier for everyone.

Beth was furious at the pain that she experienced during delivery, furious that her doctor would not give her total anesthesia, furious that her husband wasn't doing more to help. In the throes of a contraction, she screamed that she hated her husband and swore that she would never allow him to touch her again. Obviously, she did not mean any of the things she was saying. In fact, she didn't even remember saying them and was very embarrassed when she was told what had happened.

While every woman does not become a screaming lunatic in the delivery room, it might be a good idea for you and your husband to reach a truce before you even begin. You should really make a point of telling him that you love him and that he shouldn't take anything said in labor as an accurate representation of your true feelings. This is not a time when you are required to be in control of your emotions. It may help you and your husband if you do let it all hang out, however absurd it may sound.

CONGRATULATIONS. IT'S A . . .

At last, you're a mother. Your first feeling will probably be one of tremendous relief that the pain has ended. Your second feeling will be concern for the health and well-being of the infant. What happens after that runs the full gamut of emotions, none of which you could have planned for or anticipated, or even made sense of. Some typical reactions are:

- ❦ "Oh, I really wanted a girl, are you sure it's a boy." While your husband is yelling, "It's a boy. It's a boy."

- ❦ "What do you mean twins. I'm not having twins."

- ❦ "That's not my baby. It looks like a little monkey."

- ❦ "Why doesn't he stop crying. Why are you hitting him? If he keeps crying, he'll choke. He's turning blue."

- ❦ "Are you sure she's okay. You're sure, she's okay. She's so quiet."

- ❦ "I'm going to sleep. I'm exhausted. I'll deal with this later."

- ❦ "We did it. We did it. I can't believe it. The two of us made this beautiful baby."

DIFFICULT BIRTHS AND DEFECTS

It is not unusual for there to be some minor problems with labor. Many women experience difficulties such as their water breaking early or the need to induce labor or an unexpected cesarean delivery. Plan though you might, nature sometimes throws you a curve. This is why you have taken care to choose an obstetrician you trust, someone who can think quickly and knows the latest medical procedures.

One of the most difficult issues you hopefully will

never have to face is what to do in the event of a potentially life-threatening situation. Unfortunately, bad things do happen, even to mothers who have taken every precaution possible to protect their developing baby and have no knowledge of any congenital problems before conceiving. Because of this, your doctor must know before the delivery to what extreme you will go to preserve a child born with serious health problems.

This is an extremely personal issue. One that you should decide based on your religious beliefs, your feelings as a couple, and your financial and emotional ability to sustain a sick infant. It is also a decision you can only make after careful medical diagnostics. Before you know what the best thing is to do for your baby, you should have a complete medical picture of the condition, the prognosis for survival, and the impact on the child's life.

Marisa gave birth to a four-week premature baby. An hour after delivery, the baby experienced heart failure. They were in a rural hospital and the diagnostic equipment was not sophisticated enough to determine what or how serious the problem was. For eight terrifying hours, they watched doctors and nurses struggle to keep the baby alive while they tried to find a hospital that could do the proper diagnostic work. The baby was helicoptered to a university hospital. Before the baby was moved, Marisa and John had to decide what the doctor should do if the tests revealed that the baby's likelihood of survival was slim. Thankfully, Ginny is now two years old, very healthy and very happy.

This brings us to the issue of home delivery and whether or not to have an obstetrician or a mid-wife. While this all sounds so natural and feminist, it is a choice that should be made after taking your physical history, the distance to a good hospital, and the stability of your pregnancy into careful consideration. While most deliveries are extremely normal, there are no guarantees. If you are in a hospital, you have available to you the most advanced medical equipment to save and prevent any possible damage to you or your child.

Try to maintain some perspective on what is happening to the two of you, that it is happening to both of you together, that it is no one person's fault, and you shouldn't waste a minute trying to cast blame. Blame will only negatively affect your relationship and hold you back. You need to move forward now, to help each other to heal. There is enough stress in your life now that you have a newborn infant. You don't have to add further stress by arguing over how you behaved during labor and delivery.

WHY DON'T I FEEL HAPPY?

There are many myths surrounding what a woman is supposed to feel immediately after struggling for hours to push an infant out of her body and into the world. One of the most damaging is that you are at this moment happier than you've ever been in your life, your body and soul swelling with maternal love.

Many women feel nothing but exhaustion after delivery, take a quick look at the baby, and fall asleep. Of course, what you feel at this moment is in direct correlation to how long and difficult your delivery has been. The amount of pain you have experienced for such an extraordinary length of time is enough to make your post-delivery mood less than perfect.

Pat, who was in labor for 36 hours with her first child, found it very difficult to feel delighted and thrilled when the doctor presented her with a screaming child. All she wanted to do was go to sleep and said as much. When her husband came to visit after her nap, he found her crying.

I felt so guilty and ashamed that I didn't want to be with my baby from the minute she was born. I thought that the doctor and nurses probably thought I was a heartless mother.

First of all, don't concern yourself with what the doctor and nurses think. Second, don't feel guilty. You deserve and need the nap. You are exhausted enough at this point to not be able to face anything. And, as we said before, you cannot be held responsible for your performance in the delivery room.

WHY IS IT TAKING SO LONG?

One of the other things that will play on your mind while you're going through an extremely long labor is the fear that it's taking so long because something is wrong. Unfortunately, there's no way anyone can really assure you that anything isn't wrong. Take comfort in the fact that for the duration of your labor you are hooked up to all sorts of monitors. The baby's health is carefully watched. If your baby is in distress, the doctor would move immediately to do a cesarean section. Modern medical practice dictates that as long as all vital signs are healthy, mom just has to tough it out.

This isn't just a decision made for good medical reasons, but for legal reasons, too. Obstetricians are in one of the most vulnerable areas of medical practice these days. They try not to do anything radical enough to ire their patient, and they don't take risks.

Long before this stage, you should have learned your

doctor's position on cesareans, and he should know yours. A doctor who is overly anxious to do cesareans is just as dangerous as one overly reluctant to do one.

OUT FOR THE COUNT

Despite trends toward natural childbirth, there are women who do not want to be awake during the delivery, who want to deliver by appointment and under anesthesia, who do not want any pain associated with labor. There are also husbands who cannot bear to see their wives suffer during labor, cannot stand the sight of blood, the smell of a hospital room, and cannot under any circumstances be in the delivery room.

If you do decide to have a scheduled delivery, or if due to some possible danger to your baby, your doctor determines that it would be best to induce labor and deliver surgically, you should still schedule some time for you and your husband to share the delivery experience. Your husband may be able to stay in the room during the cesarean delivery. He can certainly wait with you while the anesthesia takes affect. At the very least he should be waiting for you in the recovery room and have full details to report once the anesthesia has worn off.

HONEY, I CAN'T HANDLE THIS

Don and Roberta had vastly differing views about the role of the father during labor. Don felt his place was in the waiting room, pacing with coffee and cigarettes, and finally seeing his wife and child when the screams, grunts, and bleeding were over. Roberta knew that Don felt this way before she delivered. Don had been telling her he felt this way throughout her pregnancy. Despite all of this, and the fact that Roberta knew Don had major difficulties facing anybody in pain, Roberta grew extremely angry with Don. She held on to her anger right through the delivery and into her first visit with her husband, almost ruining her marriage and the joy that she and Don both felt at having this beautiful child.

Roberta had been attracted to Don because of his sensitivity and soft touch, but now she saw this trait in a negative light. Would he ever be there for her when things got bad, when she got sick, when the baby got sick? He only seemed to be able to handle life when everyone was happy. He even tried to smooth out their latest crisis with his typical put-on-a-happy-face attitude toward life. This threw Roberta into a rage.

While this was not the best time to have to face this problem, Roberta was confronting what she considered to be a serious stumbling block in her marriage. She could not be the one to soldier through the tough times while Don stuck his head in the sand. She needed to know that she wasn't out there alone, and the way Don managed this delivery was concrete proof that she was. Roberta felt that Don was going to have to change, and if he had to go to therapy to do it, well that was what he was going to have to do.

Cynthia, however, was able to accept Herman's unwillingness to participate in her labor. As a child, Herman was always blamed for any pain his parents or siblings suffered. Even if his younger brother fell in the street, Herman was to blame for not watching him carefully. When Cynthia was in pain or unhappy, Herman was preconditioned to believe that it was his fault. As they were going through the prenatal classes, Herman confessed his fear that watching Cynthia in the torment of labor would cause him so much guilt that he would never be able to have sex with her again. Cynthia respected Herman's situation and agreed to begin therapy with him a few months after the baby was born.

REST UP

These days the average post-delivery hospital stay is only three days. Take advantage of it. This will be the last time you can sleep as long as you like for months to come. You should also use the opportunity to share some time with your husband. Maybe he can scrounge some extra vacation days, or leave early every afternoon. It's nice to be together for those first feedings and to have the luxury to cover all the last-minute details before you go home.

Just as we insist on your husband sharing in the delivery, don't forget the other children at home. Keep them abreast of everything that's happening. Have them come to visit you in the hospital. Most hospitals allow Mommy to come to the waiting room or admissions area. Most hospitals also take a picture of your baby seconds after birth. If your children aren't old enough to see the baby in the nursery, let them see the picture.

These early visits can go a long way toward easing the adjustment to a new baby at home. Bring presents for your older children, encourage them to buy a little gift for the new baby, ask them what they want to do as soon as the baby comes home, and, of course, make them tell you all the details of their days while you're in the hospital positive aspects of being a big brother or a big sister.

Your husband can also take on the role of social director. You will be swamped by people anxious to visit you and to get an early peak at your new baby. This is a time when you both need to feel that others are sharing your joy, but it's also a time when you don't want to confront people who could present problems.

Let people send flowers, hand out cigars, mail cards, and visit as long as you can handle it. Who comes to the hospital is really up to you. You may want to restrict visiting to immediate family members or just share most of the time with each other. By all means, feel free to tell well-wishers that you'd rather not have visitors and would rather they come to visit a week or so after you get home. Once again, what you can manage in the way of visiting is directly tied to your mood after delivery.

Don't call the people you think will be a problem. You can notify them of the delivery after you're home and settled. Don't be afraid to be honest with people at this time. And if you can't be honest, just blame it on exhaustion and your postpartum mood. You are somewhat vulnerable to negative feelings right now. Your hormones are still bouncing around and out of balance, you need support and positive nurturing. If a visitor can't provide that, then they shouldn't be at the hospital right now.

NOW I'M REALLY SCARED

The closer it gets to going-home time, the more nervous you may get. Babies do not come with instruction manuals, and just how much you don't know will now become extremely evident to you. Take the time to talk to the doctor and the nurses. With luck, you will have read a few child-care books during your pregnancy. If not, start cramming now, and always keep in mind that billions of people less qualified than you have raised healthy, normal children.

Some women find a newborn infant more frightening than others. If the baby is particularly small or fragile, your fear might be greater than if you gave birth to an eight-pounder. There are many deep-seated emotions behind this fear, some of which we have touched on in earlier chapters of this book. The primary motivation behind this fear, however, is just the realization of the awesome responsibility you have assumed. All of the doubts you had before you even conceived resurface. You may be sitting in your hospital room fidgeting to find some relief from your stitches, feeding your baby, when you suddenly ask yourself, "What have I done?"

This is perfectly normal. The best medicine we can prescribe is to keep close to your husband, get reinforcement and trust your own judgment about how to care for your baby. This is all part of the postpartum experience. We will deal with this in greater detail in the following chapters.

READY?

It is hoped that all is ready at home. The room has been painted and decorated, hired help is ready to start on schedule, hubby has stocked the refrigerators and cupboards, and the place has been cleaned while you've been recovering. The last thing you need to walk into is a chaotic mess. If you know your husband is not the tidy type, make arrangements for cleaning help to come in just before you go home.

COMING HOME AND THE FIRST WEEK AT HOME

It's a joyous time. It's a frightening time. You've been lying in a hospital bed for three days, resting, visiting, administering to your baby with the help of the nurses. Then, one morning, your husband arrives with a bunch of flowers and fresh clothes. You dress. The nurses come in with your baby, an orderly brings a wheelchair. You wave good-bye—amazed at how close you've come to feel with the staff and your roommates—and within minutes you're out the door, into a waiting cab or car, and on your way home to assume the role of full-time mother.

WHAT ARE YOU FEELING RIGHT NOW?

Well, you're probably happy, excited, proud, and full of hope and expectation. And, you definitely feel, and are probably voicing these sentiments, that you never want to be pregnant again. For most new mothers, even those want-

159

ing several children, the memory of pregnancy and delivery is too vividly gruesome to make them anxious for a repeat performance. For most people, this too does pass. You may also be feeling frightened, insecure, overwhelmed, panicked, and a little depressed right now. These negative feelings are quite common to all new parents, nothing to be ashamed of, but certainly something that must be brought out into the open and expressed before they have a negative effect on you and your new family.

WHAT ARE YOU AFRAID OF?

The answer is, plenty. It is very unlikely that you will ever confront any one more dependent on you than a newborn infant. Your newborn infant's life is truly in your hands. You have an awesome power. You are responsible for every aspect of this infant's physical and emotional well-being. And, as we all know, babies don't come with instruction manuals. So, if you're frightened you have good reason to be.

Your obstetrician can answer many of your questions about caring for an infant. Most doctors also provide their patients with a recommended reading list of expert child-care books that outline a baby's physical and psychological development. Your obstetrician will also refer you to a pediatrician. Family and friends with children are also a good source of advice, so you aren't quite as alone in this as you may think.

For most people, love and instinct triumph over anxiety, and they overcome their initial fear. They do not, however, ever stop worrying about their child and their performance as parents. Worry seems to come with your new job description.

WELCOME HOME

If you went into delivery well-prepared, the baby's room will be ready, a live-in or part-time baby nurse hired, the refrigerator will be stocked, the house cleaned, and grandparents will be waiting to help. You and your husband will also have established a plan of attack, detailing who will do what as you try to establish a routine. And, hopefully, you both will have read this chapter before leaving the hospital.

The first thing you should have decided upon is who will be waiting when you get home. Many new mothers come home to find their entire extended family, neighbors, friends, and a catered party waiting for them. While this is undoubtedly a sign of how excited everyone is for you, this may not be the homecoming you need. It takes a newborn infant some time to become adjusted to its environment and to its mother. Being passed from person to person may overwhelm your baby. It's true that a newborn infant can't do much, but it can take an awful lot in and this level of excitement may just be too much. Not to mention that you probably don't look or feel too ready to clean up after a mob of well-wishers. So the nicest homecoming may be the low-key homecoming. Give yourself at least a day or so to adjust before inviting everyone over.

If you're smart, you'll let the people who are waiting for you make your first day at home easier. If your parents are waiting, let them keep an eye on the baby while you take a warm shower, do your hair, make yourself pretty and comfortable. They're excited about the baby. Let them fuss over the baby while you take a minute to rest and take care of yourself. Put your feet up. They can take care of their own food. Let them change the first few diapers. There will be plenty of dirty diapers for you to change, plenty of time to do things your way. Try to sneak in a little nap while they're visiting. You may not get another opportunity for uninterrupted sleep for a long time.

THE BEST LAID PLANS OF MOM AND DAD

Sometimes, however, all the planning in the world doesn't bring the result you'd hoped for. This is why you and your husband should at the very least feel confident in your mutual support. If you do get home to a house full of partying friends, don't blow up, don't blame each other. Let everyone have a quick look at your baby. If your husband is in the mood to celebrate, let him. Then explain to your guests that you and the baby need a rest. Play host or leave that role to your parents. Once again, do what makes you both feel comfortable. If you aren't exhausted and you feel like having a party, by all means, join in.

THE MYTHS ABOUT CHILDBIRTH

- Now that you've delivered, you'll be the happiest mother and father in the world.

- You will feel a deep emotional bond and love, and adore your baby instantly.

- All your feelings toward your new child will be positive. Any negative feelings are hideous and should be suppressed.

- Only women experience postpartum depression.

- The pain of labor ends with the delivery.

- You'll be back on your feet, back on the job, back to your former weight in no time.

- ❦ Anybody can breastfeed. It comes naturally.

- ❦ Your life will pick up just where it left off. You can have it all.

- ❦ Your older children will hate the new baby.

SHATTERING THE MYTHS: A REALISTIC APPROACH

The sad thing about myths is that while there is some truth to them, they generally oversimplify everything and become destructive to those people who don't fit the broad generalization. It's true. You will undoubtedly both be very hopeful, positive, and happy about your new infant, but those aren't the only feelings you will be experiencing.

First of all, you are still under the influence of very powerful and uncontrollable hormonal changes, so your feelings will change rapidly and seemingly without rhyme or reason. Your husband, although not victim to the hormonal influences, will also fall victim to the emotional ups and downs common after any long-awaited, major life experience.

After nine months of waiting, fantasy, and anticipation, reality can at first be a bit of a letdown. This doesn't mean that you aren't delighted with the baby. You are only human and all that anticipation and planning is exhausting. The best cure for this depression is to just take the time to relax and grow accustomed to your life.

THIS ISN'T MY BABY

Another aspect of the deliriously happy myth is that you will have an immediate love affair with your baby. Yes, most of the time you will gaze at your infant with blind adoration, but there will be moments when you are absolutely convinced that you've been given the wrong baby, that you don't even like this baby, and that the whole idea of being a mother or father is distasteful and annoying. No one can truly anticipate how they will feel about their new baby before the actual arrival. That's why mutual support, openness, and understanding are critical to your relationship at this time.

> *We were both changing the baby's diapers when, all of a sudden, I thought, "He's so ugly. How did I get into this? I don't want him at all." I started to cry. Carl asked me what was wrong. I was too ashamed to tell him. I cried in his arms like a baby. He kept assuring me that whatever I felt was okay. He just wanted me to talk to him. Finally, I could bring myself to voice what I was feeling. He just held me, smiled, and repeated over and over again that I was beautiful, the baby was beautiful. I guess he kind of loved me out of it.*

A newborn infant, no matter how beautiful, scarcely has enough personality to provoke any negative feelings. So, where do these feelings come from? Most of your negative feelings have nothing to do with your baby, and everything to do with your fears and anxieties about your ability to be a parent. They are a total transference of your fear of responsibility and failure, your anxieties about your marriage, and in some cases, anger at the way you were raised by your parents.

A woman left totally fatigued by delivery and overwhelmed by her new role, for example, may become irrationally angry that her husband can now have all the joy of fatherhood without having endured any of the pain of labor.

A sensitive spouse can help by allowing his wife to voice her anger and then reassuring her that he appreciates what she has been through and loves her for it. This is particularly important if he was not in the delivery room.

THE GREEN-EYED MONSTER

Strange as it seems, parental jealousy is also a feeling that can be transferred to the baby. If the baby is now getting all of its mother's attention, if daddy is not part of the feeding or changing, if all the friends are doting on the baby, daddy can feel pretty left out. If this jealousy and the postpartum letdown so many men feel gets out of hand, it could interfere with the cementing of a positive father-child and marital relationship. In fact, your spouse may begin to feel that if he's not needed he may just as well disengage himself from the family unit. This withdrawal can be the beginning of very serious marital problems. It's an issue we will address later in greater detail.

I'M SO UNCOMFORTABLE

The physical effects of labor do not, unfortunately, pass once the baby has been pushed into the world. For starters, the muscular effort you expended to bring the baby into the world is the same as or maybe even greater than the most strenuous workout you've ever had. Think how tight and achy you feel after heavy abdominal exercises, and it only seems natural that you would experience some muscular discomfort for days after delivery.

Hemorrhoids may be another source of physical agony. The heaviness of the baby during the last trimester and the act of pushing during labor often cause women to develop hemorrhoids. Then there is the discomfort caused by the episiotomy. The stitches to close the incision take a long time to heal. Getting up and down from a chair, walking, and urinating may be extremely painful until the stitches dissolve or are removed. Even the sitz bath that your doctor prescribes may not relieve all of your pain.

Hormone changes do take a physical as well as emotional toll at this time. After delivery and until you stop breastfeeding, you will have an elevated progesterone level. This post-delivery hormone causes vaginal dryness and irritation, and adds to your overall discomfort.

GRIN AND BEAR IT

Now that there's a baby at home, you can't curl up in bed and sleep until all the pain passes. A hungry baby does not understand that your stitches are bothering you, so you must lie down. This is when your predelivery planning pays off. It is hoped that you have help—even if it's just a friend or family member who comes in for a few hours a day.

NO SEX, PLEASE, WE'RE PARENTS

Your doctor will have advised you that sex, until at least six weeks after delivery, is out of the question. Mind you, with all the discomfort you are feeling, sex is the last thing you would want. However, as we recommended in earlier chapters, abstaining from sex does not mean abstaining from affection, touching, physical intimacy, or meeting your partner's needs in some mutually agreeable manner. Physical intimacy can go a long way toward soothing the emotional and physical upheaval of these first days of parenthood. It helps to reinforce your sense of loving partnership and mutual support.

MIRROR, MIRROR

Even if you were a fanatic about your weight before and during your pregnancy, it will take time for your body to get back to normal after delivery. Most doctors do not recommend immediately returning to strenuous physical exercise or strict dieting right after delivery. It can take months to regain your shape. If you are breastfeeding, it may take even longer. Your body needs the extra food and weight to produce milk to feed your baby. Talk to your doctor. There are many weight control programs available for nursing mothers, and your doctor will be able to assess which program will be healthiest for you. Once again, do not expect or strive for a dramatic drop in your weight. You will slowly and surely return to your normal body weight if you follow a reasonable program.

If you really blew your diet during your pregnancy, you've got an even tougher battle ahead of you. Weight put on during pregnancy is not easily lost, and will power isn't an easy thing to muster when you're struggling with a newborn. But the weight should be lost. It is important for your self-image and your marriage. Most men need visual stimulation to feel sexually aroused. And, you both need to know that having a child has not transformed two passionate lovers into something you swore you'd never become—an asexual mommy and daddy.

OUT FOR THE COUNT

Even when you start to look like your old self, don't be surprised if you still feel like you couldn't go ten rounds with a limp noodle. You don't recover from nine months of pregnancy and hours of labor in a few days. A long restful vacation would be a godsend right now. No such luck. You are about to embark on a life of late-night feedings and little or no sleep—a period so exhausting that it is commonly described as a fog. Many new parents claim that they are so fatigued, so out of their normal rhythm that they can barely differentiate one day from the next. So, what's a new mother to do.

Zak was so happy to have me at home again. It was funny. He was the one who was always zipping around the globe on business. So many times, I would tell him that I wished he didn't travel because I missed him so much, but he couldn't understand it. I was only in the hospital for three days, but the way he carried on when I got home, you would have thought it was a month. He had so many plans for us. We were going to have our parents over on the first night. Good friends on the weekend. He was going to take me out shopping for things to keep me busy while I was home with the baby. He wanted me to bring the baby in to his office right after her first doctor's visit.

I had to tell him that I just didn't know if I could keep up with his plans. The man looked destroyed. "But, you're not pregnant anymore," he said. "It's the old you, again." It was then that I realized that it wasn't only the three days that had thrown Zak, but that he had truly missed me for a full nine months. He needed me to be available to him.

The best way to feel close to your husband, to take some of the pressure off yourself, and to give him a very clear idea of why you feel the way you do is to involve him in every aspect of the baby's routine. Let your husband share in the 1 A.M. and 3 A.M. feedings. This may seem like a punishment, but when he has to get up for work three hours after a feeding, he will begin to understand how exhausting motherhood can be.

NO COMPARISONS

We all know some superwoman who delivered her baby on a Friday, looked like she'd never been pregnant by Saturday, and was back at work in three weeks or less. Well this is a rare woman and not a standard to which you should be comparing yourself. The truth is you shouldn't compare yourself to anyone. As we have stated throughout this book, every pregnancy is different, even in terms of the amount of time it takes for you to get back into the swing of things.

YOUR DESK IS WAITING

Chances are good that during the first week after delivery, the thought of going back to work will hardly be a top priority. It may, in fact, seem that the job you left only weeks ago existed in a different lifetime. You and your husband should, however, start thinking about when and if you will return to work. It is likely that your employer may now start asking about your estimated day of return, too.

While finances may largely determine when you must return to your job, your physical and emotional needs should play a large part in this decision, too.

Try to negotiate for as much paid leave as you possibly can. Ask about using your vacation days as part of your paid maternity leave. It is really a good idea to spend as much time as you can with your newborn baby.

If you are truly exhausted, you are doing no one, least of all yourself, a favor by quickly returning to work. Your job will suffer. Your baby will suffer, and so will your marriage. An overtired person is often an angry, unproductive, and depressed person.

In any case, now is the time to be making plans, not to

be running for the train. Just try to think clearly and do what's necessary and best for your family.

Staying at home with your baby will give you the opportunity to really get to know your child and help to build your confidence as a mother. And, it goes a long way toward rebuilding your strength.

THE CURSE OF MOTHERHOOD

Guilt. Yes, it starts right at the beginning. Every time you make a decision you worry that you've made the right one. This is particularly true in making the decision to go back to work. Even the most hard-boiled career-driven business woman will feel that she should be home with her baby. Again, the longer you can stay at home, the less guilt you will feel about abandoning your baby. Of course, if earning a salary is your overriding concern right now, you should take comfort in the fact that providing an income is equally important to your child's well-being. You are doing the best you can, and there is nothing wrong with that.

THIS IS NOT BUSINESS AS USUAL

Melissa had worked as a literary agent for six years before she had her baby. She had a large comfortable apartment with plenty of room for a new baby and an office. She and her husband, John, had spent months before the new baby's arrival organizing Melissa's new at-home office, mailing out change-of-address cards, and dreaming about how Melissa would be back to work in no time.

I felt good after Jill was born, a little tired, but I'd had a pretty smooth delivery. Lying there in the hospital I really had no doubts that my plan to go back to work in two, at the most three, weeks would come off without a hitch. Fat chance. I've got my biggest author on the phone. The baby's screaming. She's hungry. It doesn't matter to her that I'm noodling the finishing touches on a deal. So, I balance the phone on my shoulder, pop my breast in her mouth, and try to do business. Hopeless, totally hopeless. And forget about reading manuscripts. It's impossible when you haven't had more than three hours sleep. After a month of trying to make a go of it, we decided to hire a part-time nurse. At least then, I could get some sleep and schedule work hours for when I had some help.

As Melissa's story illustrates, life does not pick up just where it left off. It may be difficult for you to accept less from yourself, but if you can't take life back in the fast lane, you're going to have to get used to it for awhile. You'll get up to speed in your own good time. Push yourself beyond what you can healthfully manage and you will become more fatigued and require more time to recuperate. Also, setting unrealistic expectations for yourself, will only go to undermine your confidence in your ability to mother.

As painful as it may be for you to accept, what you considered to be your normal life isn't your normal life anymore. Your focus has shifted. You are now living for your baby and will continue to do so until your baby doesn't need to feed every two hours, sleeps through the night, and can entertain itself.

Just as you may want to get things right back on track, so might your husband. In fact, those husbands who don't spend time alone as the sole caretaker of their infant may not even understand how you could possibly be as tired as you are. Debbie's husband, Paul, for example, worried that she would have too much time on her hands and be bored at home all day. Prior to the baby's arrival, his job as a successful entertainment lawyer had kept them both very busy. Now that Debbie could no longer accompany him on his late-night club crawls, he thought it might be nice to surprise her and invite some people over for dinner.

> *At 5:00 P.M. I was still in my pajamas. The baby had been crying all day. Every time I laid him down, he would just start in. The only thing that seemed to help was feeding him. I swear, I think he was breastfeeding every two hours that day. When Paul came home, I hid in the bedroom. When he came in the room, he almost died. We had a major rock and roll artist and his wife in the living room, and I was still in my flannels. I had to keep my cool. Paul really thought he was doing something wonderful for me. I wanted to strangle him. I handed him the baby, a menu from a very good restaurant that delivers, and told him to play it by ear for a half hour. It turned out to be a fun evening, but we had a major discussion the next morning.*

The lesson to be learned by Debbie and Paul's experience is that both parents really need to develop a good understanding of what it's like to spend a day at home alone with the baby. You can't really scream at a person who doesn't know what baby care involves and is really trying to brighten your day out of kindness and love. So, ask your husband to take a day off, or schedule a Saturday to leave to do whatever it is you want, while he stays home with the baby. When you then sit down and explain to him that you think it might be a good idea to forget about having dinner guests or after-work surprise visitors for a while, he'll understand.

SIBLING RIVALRY, PART II

Joe really worried about what Susan and Billy would feel when he broke the news that I'd had a baby girl. After he left the hospital, he stopped off at a toystore and must have bought at least one of everything. When the kids came home, he told them the presents were for them. Mommy had a girl and he wanted to congratulate them on their new sister. Susan beamed. Bruce who was really too little to understand whispered to Susan, "Maybe if Mommy has another baby, I can get a new bike."

"Oooh, watch out for the other children," your old aunt Sadie says. "They have so much trouble with a new baby." Just because everybody spouts this kind of wisdom, it doesn't necessarily make it true. How your children will handle the arrival of a new sibling has everything to do with how secure you make them feel about the change that is about to come, and how old they are.

A confident child of seven will most likely take the new baby in stride. They have already made something of a break from mom and dad. You can, however, expect a two-year-old or even a five-year-old child to be very jealous. They still believe that they are the center of their parent's universe and don't understand this intruder. They may express these feelings by ignoring you when you're available to them, and then making unreasonable demands on you as soon as your attention is on the baby. Sometimes a very well-behaved child will turn into a monster overnight, trying to get any attention even if it's negative. Your child may act out this jealousy in his play. Chuckie, for example, circled his new sister's crib with his G.I. Joe dolls enacting an attack on the evil enemy. Michael would cry when visitors who used to always play with him came over and wanted to hold his little brother.

What's the best course of action? Let your actions speak for themselves. Include your older children in all the events of the new baby's life and the family decisions concerning the new baby. Reinforce the idea that the family is bigger now, and therefore better, and that every one of your children plays an important role. The position of big brother or sister is very attractive if it's presented as enhancing the older child's place in the family.

ALL GROWN UP

Do not, however, under any circumstances make your older children feel that their new position excludes them from any further childish feelings or behavior. The new position should not be presented as one of enormous responsibility or the beginning of adulthood. Too much responsibility is unfair and frightening to a child.

DON'T PUSH IT

Don't tell your child he or she must love the new baby. If you force your child into expressing feelings he doesn't necessarily feel, he may respond with resistance and outright hostility. The positive feelings will come naturally with time.

WE'RE HERE

No matter how tired you are, you must make yourself available to your older children. Pay extra attention to their needs. Ask your child what he or she would like to do on a Saturday or after school, and then carry through the special plan. Maybe they have something special that they would like to do with or for the new baby. Let them go ahead with it. This all reinforces that the older child is now a more important part of the family. Tell guests who come to visit the new baby to make a point of including the older child in the excitement, to treat him or her like a little celebrity, and reinforce the notion that since the older child has known them longer, he or she is their special friend. Remember, if your children feel safe and loved in the family, they will accept the new arrival happily.

THE BABY ISN'T ALWAYS THE PROBLEM

Robert was four years old when his mother came home with his new baby sister. Right from the outset he was not happy about the idea. He was extremely jealous, negative, and exhibited near violent behavior when any attention was shown to the baby. Beryl and Ron, quite rightly, sought professional help. Through family therapy sessions it was soon made painfully clear that Robert, who was an extremely overindulged first child, was also an extremely overstressed child. As a very bright first child, Robert was pushed into a demanding preschool and under a great deal of pressure to perform. The new baby only meant more pressure, more responsibility, and less attention for him, and he didn't want any part of it.

Beryl and Ron quickly realized that Robert needed some help. They had to make some major adjustments in their family life. First, Robert was placed in a less intense preschool program closer to home for fewer hours a day. Ron, who spent most of his time at the office, began to schedule evenings and afternoons with his young son. Little by little Robert began to feel more comfortable about his position in the family and was able to accept his younger sibling.

WHAT HELPS?

You may feel like you're stumbling around in the dark with no idea of where to go or what to do and that your life has become nothing more than hard work, sleepless nights, and uncertainty, but do not despair. There are some things that can make it a little easier.

BELIEVE IN YOURSELF

Many new parents have a tendency to mistrust their own instincts and believe that everyone else's advice is right. Your mother and mother-in-law, aunts, uncles, and great-grandparents all have an opinion about how your baby should be raised and will be more than willing to share this information with you. Many older people tend to believe that since they have already raised their children, regardless of how their children have turned out, they are experts and know better than you do.

They will gladly tell you that whatever knowledge you have comes from books, and babies don't operate by books. Keep in mind that the extent to which the person giving the advice will try to undermine all your good intentions is directly related to how confident they are about themselves. Parents who seem to have no confidence in their children are generally acting out their lack of belief in themselves. If you can remember that, it may become easier to ignore what you don't want or need to hear. Share your worries and mistakes only with those people who won't treat you like a fool. And most important, always present an image of a husband and wife united in mutual beliefs and support.

WHOOPS, I MADE A MISTAKE

Now, mistakes are nothing to be ashamed of. They happen to every new parent. They are all part of learning. Anybody can put a bootie on the wrong way, confuse a feeding schedule, or even sleep through the baby's afternoon bottle. Babies are sturdier than they look, and little mistakes aren't going to cause any long-term problems. You do, in fact, quickly develop a sense of what your baby wants and needs, what it likes to eat, what doesn't agree with it, and you will definitely know when your baby is hungry. If you are breastfeeding, your body quickly adapts to the baby's feeding schedule. Your breasts are uncomfortably full by the time of the next feeding, and when the baby starts to cry for food they may automatically begin to leak milk.

WHY IS THE BABY CRYING?

This is one of life's biggest questions. Why? Because so many times there is no answer, or no answer that reasonable parents can figure out. Babies cry. Sometimes there is a reason for it. Sometimes they are in distress and need your help. Sometimes they just cry for no reason at all. And, that's the crying that can send new parents into a real panic.

First of all, no one likes to hear a baby cry. It hurts emotionally, and it doesn't do a lot for your ears or nerves. Any good parent will do their best to find the source of their child's crying and stop it. If there doesn't seem to be any easy solution to the problem, parental anxiety levels can really skyrocket.

I was home alone. Greg was out of town on business. Well, Alan started crying at about 2 A.M. I fed him and he quieted down a bit. When I tried to put him back in the crib, he just started wailing again. I thought he must still be hungry, so I tried feeding him some more. He didn't want it. The crying got worse. I walked the floor all night. By 9 A.M., when the doctor's office opened, I was in a real state. I called, told the nurses what was going on. They ran through a list of questions—did I check this, check that, look at his feet, his hands. I did it all. There didn't seem to be anything wrong, but he was still crying. I called Greg in Seattle. He didn't know what to do, so I dressed the baby for a trip to the doctor, convinced there was something really seriously wrong. We weren't out the door ten seconds and Alan was quiet. I know this sounds nuts, but the next time he started crying like that, I held him for a while, then dressed him, put him in the carriage, and walked around the backyard. It worked.

Babies sometimes don't make sense to adults. Anne did the right thing. She called her doctor and got expert advice. Long crying spells are unpleasant and can signify larger problems. They also can be totally meaningless. You will quickly learn enough about your baby to ascertain when something is wrong and when it's just making noise.

WHY ISN'T THE BABY CRYING?

Marilyn and Jason had just had their second child and were expecting that the first week would be a repeat performance of their experience with Ben—up all night walking the floor, long crying spells. Well, it just didn't happen that way. Little Jennifer barely made a peep and slept for four to five hours at a time. Marilyn began to worry that there was something wrong with her baby daughter and called a friend. Her friend consoled her with the story that her first child had also been a very quiet, well-behaved baby, so quiet, in fact, that she would sometimes forget she was in the house until she started to cry. Every baby is different, and being quiet just like crying, is no indication of a problem. This story reinforces just how worrisome and uncertain the first few weeks and months of a new baby's life can be. You know so little about babies, in general, and your baby, in particular, that it's very easy to worry about anything that happens—good or bad.

PARENTS ARE PEOPLE, TOO

The bottom line is that if your heart is in the right place, and you really love your child, you will do the right thing, even if you're not sure what the right thing is at the time. It may be extremely hard to sit there and watch your baby cry. You can imagine your child a grown adult unburdening themselves to a therapist, claiming you didn't love them enough because you didn't always pick him up when he cried. Guilt solves no problems. You really can only do your best, learn from what's going on, and show your children how much they are loved.

YOU MUST BREASTFEED

After years of embarrassment, breastfeeding is suddenly out in the open and in vogue. Everybody thinks they have to breastfeed. Friends, family, and medical professionals are pushing breastfeeding as the only thing to do. Well that just isn't so. How you choose to feed your baby is your business and certainly does not reflect on the quality of mothering you are providing. You do what you can and what you and your baby feel comfortable with. Many women cannot breastfeed for medical reasons—their breasts simply do not manufacture enough or healthy milk—or find the experience physically unpleasant. Many babies don't like to be breastfed.

Don't succumb to the pressure of friends and family who may tell you that you're depriving your child of important antibodies, or that breastfeeding is psychologically better for the baby. If you can't breastfeed or don't want to, it doesn't make you less of a woman.

THE BABY NURSE

This is the one person who can be your savior or your nemesis during the first week at home. Hopefully you've taken enough time to find someone who will fit comfortably into your family unit, someone who complements your style, someone you can communicate with, and someone who responds and respects both of you.

Ina and Arthur had negotiated for months to get the baby nurse all their friends recommended. Everyone in their building raved about Clara. She was British, competent, and a paragon of efficiency. The new parents felt blessed to have her waiting when they brought the new baby home. Within an hour of her arrival, Clara had organized the baby's room, the bathroom, had a full stock of diapers, and her clothes neatly and inconspicuously tucked away in a closet.

At first Ina and Arthur felt relieved that they were in such secure and steady hands. Within two days Clara had transformed their house into a baby hospital, had the baby on a strict schedule, and left mother and father feeling totally helpless around their own child. Their apartment was now her apartment, and their baby was her baby. They were only allowed to spend a prescheduled number of supervised hours a day with the baby. And, since Clara supervised these sessions there was no time for spontaneous fun.

At the end of the third day with Clara, Ina and Arthur decided something had to be done. Clara had to go. They would take care of their baby alone until they could find someone who didn't make them feel like invaders in their own home. Clara was not happy when she was dismissed. She informed the new parents that they were so inept at handling their baby that they'd certainly ruin the child.

Some of what Clara said really alarmed Ina and Arthur. They knew they had a lot to learn, but they also recognized that they had each other and could learn together. A baby nurse like Clara was not going to create the loving home they both wanted for their child, and they would just have to muddle through on their own.

Max and Cynthia were not quite as lucky as Ina and Arthur. Their baby nurse experience nearly turned traumatic. Without consulting Cynthia, Max went out and hired Sophia, the Italian baby nurse his mother recommended. Sophia spoke no English. Cynthia spoke no Italian. All communications regarding the baby were handled through Max, and when Cynthia was home during the day with Sophia, life was a nightmare. After five days of living with a woman who she couldn't understand but who seemed to dislike her, Cynthia had to confront Max. He was shocked to learn how threatened and miserable she felt. After a long and bitter discussion they agreed to dismiss Sophia. This sent shockwaves through their entire extended family. Max's mother was insulted and angry and put tremendous guilt on Max. He, therefore, transferred the hostility he should have been expressing toward his mother to Cynthia.

I can remember screaming at Max. "This is my baby and my house. If your mother loves Sophia so much let her have her. She could use a baby nurse!" My mother-in-law's meddling had created a huge disturbance in my family, and I hated her for it.

Eventually they abandoned the whole idea of a baby nurse and hired a housekeeper instead. Relieved of the burden of cleaning, Cynthia had more than enough time to lavish the attention she felt was needed on her son.

Your baby nurse or housekeeper must be someone you can both trust, who doesn't seem interested in getting in the middle of your marriage, who respects both husband and wife, and develops a genuine affection for your child. Both parents must be able to communicate comfortably with the nurse and neither should feel threatened or disliked. Both partners must determine the nurse's responsibilities and present a united front when there is a problem. This is not an overly confident time for many new mothers and the last thing they need is a witch or a flirt under their roof. Your baby nurse is your employee, perhaps one with whom you develop a more intimate relationship than usual, but not a girlfriend and certainly not a confidante of either you or your husband.

IT'S ALL SO NEW

During the first week, you are both still marvelling at what you've created. Everything is so new that you and your husband may not face any major baby-related confrontations. You are, however, setting the stage for how you will deal with parenting, caretaking, and the course of your relationship for the years to come.

Having a baby, as we've mentioned many times before, stirs up many long-forgotten images from our own childhoods, feelings of anger and neglect and hope that we can do better than our parents. All these old feelings begin to influence our everyday behavior as a parent and a spouse. These negative feelings are sometimes transferred to the baby, but usually they pull a husband and wife apart. That's why it is so important to step back and really understand what may be motivating the little arguments or snide remarks that are now passing between you.

ESTABLISHING A PATTERN

Your different attitudes toward child rearing will most likely present the perfect opportunity for a fight. You may believe you don't pick up the baby every time it cries. This may annoy, then anger, and then outrage your husband to the extent that you get into a real fight. These differences are the major area of conflict between parents. They cannot be ignored. You must both learn to respect each other's opinions, even though they may be different, and then find a new way to deal with your problems without fighting.

Take a look at what is making you so angry. You will probably discover that you are fighting because you are angry at how your parents raised you. Since there is nothing you can do about that now, and in fact you may never understand why it happened in your life, you are now trying to express the anger in the only way you can, by directing it at your spouse. This is pretty unproductive behavior. You do have control over your current situation and can take positive action to shape your child's life in the way you want.

Above all, when tempers heat up over the baby, do not

engage in this argument in front of the baby, and do not personalize your differences by accusing your partner of choosing one method of child rearing because he or she is not a loving parent. No matter how heated the argument may become, it should never escalate into a question of personality, character, or emotional health. Turning it into a personal issue complicates everything and inhibits the likelihood that you will both reach a resolution.

You and your spouse will have many disagreements over how to raise your child. You must find a way to manage them successfully or they will wreak havoc with your marriage. You must never accuse your husband of being stupid or inferior to you because you are, after all, the mother and know the child better. No one is stupid in these situations; things are just different. If you want to watch your relationship go down the toilet, a good way to do it is to let your spouse believe that he is an inferior parent. It will do two things: it will push him away from the child and it will push him away from you. Any problems that could have been avoided will soon escalate. When you feel the heat rising, stop and ask yourself why you are so upset about this issue. This will do two things: cool things off for a minute and reveal the true source of your anger.

The first time that Jane did not pick up the baby when he cried, Anthony began screaming that she was a neglectful mother, that she didn't really care about the baby, and that she was going to ruin the child. Anthony was truly concerned that the baby was going to suffer because he wasn't picked up. On the other hand, Jane knew that the baby was tired and just needed to whimper a little before he went to sleep. She didn't get angry at Anthony until he said Jane was just like her mother and didn't really love the baby. Jane broke out in a rage. He had pushed the wrong button and really touched on her life-long fear that she would be just like her rejecting mother. Anthony himself never realized he was overreacting because of his own feeling of having been neglected by *his* mother.

It took months of fighting and eventual therapy for Jane and Anthony to trace the source of their problems. They learned how to separate their past from their new future, and how to diffuse hostility when it seemed to be escalating out of control.

In their counseling, Jane and Anthony learned that it wasn't a bad idea to have a tape recorder around the house. Jane was in charge of bringing the tape recorder out when things started getting nuts. They would record the argument. The appearance of the recorder sometimes actually stopped the fight altogether. It was enough of a break to turn a battle in the making into a discussion. At the times that it didn't stop the fight, it did provide them with concrete evidence of just how destructive, negative, and unnecessary their behavior was. Through listening to their fights and the real issues behind the fighting, this couple was able to really break their pattern.

POSTPARTUM DEPRESSION

For years many people tried to negate the powerful emotional shift experienced by women after giving birth. The depression, the anxiety, the terror, and the potential for violence are now recognized as a real hormonal disturbance and not a self-indulgent figment of a woman's imagination. Most women do experience a hormonal depression after delivery. Don't be surprised if you feel like crying for no obvious reason, feel ambivalent about your baby, and frightened about your ability to mother a child. Your moods may swing from elation to total despair. These are all well within the realm of normal postpartum responses.

There is, unfortunately, no way to know if you are prone to extreme or dangerous hormonal depressions. Family history and your premenstrual moods are sometimes indicators that there may be a problem, but they cannot predict with total certainty. If you are worried about your feelings, talk to your doctor. If you have already had a child and experienced a deep depression, you may want to arrange for a predelivery psychiatric consultation or have the name of a psychiatrist who is an expert in postpartum problems ready should you need it.

HOW DOES THIS AFFECT YOUR MARRIAGE?

Postpartum depression can be rough on the husband. It's very hard to understand or help a person who is crying or upset for no known reason. Faced with you in this situation, your husband may experience a tremendous sense of guilt and confusion. He may begin to feel responsible for your pain and panic when he can't find a way to make it better. Try to help your husband to understand what is happening to you. He will then be able to provide the kind of support you need, know that you don't expect him to solve everything, and that you certainly don't feel he's responsible. And, since your husband knows you better than anyone else and has your best interests at heart, he can truly help you to retain a sense of balance and protect you from any harm.

HUSBANDS GET DEPRESSED, TOO

They may not suffer hormone problems, but the birth of a child can really shake up man's emotional balance. The increased responsibility and pressure of fatherhood may overwhelm him. He may feel ignored and excluded from the flurry of activity surrounding the new baby. Because he is "only" the wage earner, he may feel like a totally unnecessary member of the family. He may now feel as though he has not been successful enough in life, that he has failed at his job. Since his salary may seem to him to be the only contribution he can make to his family, this may only intensify his feelings of failure.

ONE BIG, HAPPY FAMILY

As a mother, you are in a tremendous position of power during these early days. Even though your husband may take a few days to help get everyone settled in, he will eventually return to work, and you will have the baby all to yourself all day. Your power intensifies even more if you are breastfeeding. The baby needs you more than anyone else. You are doing something for your baby that your husband can never do. It will help everyone if you organize the feedings so that your husband can become a part of them.

If you are breastfeeding, let your husband sit by your side and hold the baby's hand or talk to the baby. Many babies, particularly in the early days of life, require supplemental bottle feedings. Make those feedings something your husband does alone with his child, even if it means that he gets up for one middle-of-the-night feeding. All this goes a long way toward cementing a feeling that everyone is a participating member of the family, needed for their love not just their paycheck.

Even if your husband is uncomfortable at first, you must encourage him. Never belittle his fumbling attempts to do what after two days seems to come so naturally to you. This will convince him to never try again. And certainly don't let what you consider to be more convenient dictate who cares for the baby.

Rita, for example, insisted that she didn't mind doing everything for their infant. She claimed it was easier for her to do it herself than to take the time to explain to Howard how to do things. Now Howard was willing, uncomfortable but eager to be involved, and Rita's action just convinced him he wasn't needed or wanted. Her behavior also conveyed the message that she was the important one in their baby's life. She was very put out when a friend mentioned that she thought Rita had established a very destructive interaction with her husband. Rita didn't want to admit that she really enjoyed being the most important person in the baby's life.

There is tremendous danger in this behavior. Once you set up this sort of a family relationship, it almost always continues this way. A father who is made to feel that he is not important early in a baby's life may also assume that he is not important to his wife, can only play the role of wage earner, and will never become involved in other aspects of a child's life. He may, if his hurt is strong enough, withdraw from the family completely—first as a participating member and then through actual divorce. After all, no one wants to stay where they feel they're not wanted or needed.

As a wife and mother you should be looking toward building an equal, loving partnership with your husband, and if you're not, now's the time to sit down and examine why. Chances are pretty good the answer will be found in the pattern established by your parents. If your mother didn't give your father much credibility as a parent, you may be predisposed to act as though all men are incompetent fathers. Examine your husband's background as well. Then honestly talk about how you want to build your own life, not repeat your childhood, and make a plan. Daddy does this. Mommy does this. We all do this together. Not only will this go a long way toward making everyone feel involved, it will also help everyone to feel less exhausted, since no one person will be carrying the entire baby schedule alone.

THE BEGINNING

The first week may be early to say that this is going to be the way it is from now on, but it is certainly the time when many life-long patterns are set. If you're not happy with the way you are interacting as a couple, now's the time to do something about it—before you both become too invested in the behavior.

LITTLE PLEASURES

As negative as all this sudden transformation in your life may sound, it's important to remember that babies do grow, life does become sane again, and the love and joy you receive from your child is definitely worth these first few months of agony.

Irene and Herbert, for example, were really surprised by how quickly they forgot about the very things they swore they'd never give up after the baby came.

We were sitting in our favorite restaurant. The baby had only been home a week, but we'd sworn to each other that we wouldn't give up Saturday night dinner out just because we were parents. We could afford a live-in nurse, so there was nothing stopping us. Except ourselves that is. We talked about the baby from the minute we left the house. I think I made the first call home. We didn't even bother with dessert. We couldn't wait to get home and look at the baby again. Nuts, right? But, we were in love.

Through their efforts to maintain what they thought they really wanted, Irene and Herbert realized that they were much more emotionally attached to their baby than they ever were to their sophisticated Manhattan lifestyle. It was easy for them to stay home. In the quiet hours with their baby, they learned new things about each other and began to feel more like a family than ever before.

THE FIRST THREE MONTHS

You may feel that having survived labor, endless hospital visits, and the first week at home that you and your spouse are due for a rest. Well, you may be totally exhausted, but you still have several tough months to go.

CAN I GO TO SLEEP NOW?

If someone were to ask you what you feel right at this stage, the answer is likely to be "Exhausted. That's it. I'm too tired to feel anything else." Well, you probably haven't had a full night's sleep since you got home, so no one should be surprised by this answer. It's always best to deal with life fully rested, but, don't worry, you will manage to survive.

WHAT'S SO HARD ABOUT STAYING HOME WITH A BABY?

Well, besides the obvious hard work and exhaustion, quite a lot. First of all baby's don't talk much. They cry when they're hungry or need to be changed or just for the hell of it, and they can't tell you what's bothering them, what they're thinking, or what they want. You can't discuss the global financial crisis with them or any stimulating topic for that matter. They don't always cooperate on a shopping trip or in the movies, and they certainly aren't fun in a good restaurant. They like to stay at home all day, and they want you there with them. This pretty much eliminates your adult contacts, can confuse your identity, and leave you feeling insecure about being a contributing member of the human race.

Being an at-home, full-time mommy may have been easier when women didn't expect to do much else, but the superwoman theory and the current economic climate have blown some big holes into this as a viable lifestyle. Things are changing. More and more women are choosing to stay at home with their babies. They recognize that you can't really have it all—high-powered job, baby, and husband—and survive. Still, when we hear of a woman who has opted out of the job market, we often look at her with a mix of jealousy and shock. "How nice not to need the money," some people might think. "How nice to not need the stimulation of a job," may pop into the minds of others.

Neither one of these reasons may be behind your decision to stay home with your baby, but don't be surprised if you get some strange responses the first time you announce that you don't go out to work. The first time you go to a party and somebody asks what do you do, and you can't say you're a lawyer, nurse, writer, construction worker, or waitress, but answer that you stay home with the baby, you'll know the creeping insecurity of suspecting that all sorts of sophisticated people think you're a mindless fool. You may even begin to doubt your own sanity and intelligence.

After spending six weeks in the house watching daytime TV, I really felt like a dummy. All I could talk about were feeding schedules and diaper stories. Not exactly stimulating conversation starters for people without children. I was a little afraid to be with other women. I thought they would think I was a throwback to the dark ages. They had the excitement of their careers, a full life, a decent figure, and no baby hanging off their shoulder.

This insecurity is pretty normal and will probably pass. You have just made a major shift in how you live your life and define who you are. It will take time for you to grow accustomed to the new you. If, however, it doesn't start to feel comfortable, or if this really wasn't a decision that you made, but something that was forced on you, then you may want to reconsider. Maybe you shouldn't be a full-time mommy. Maybe you need to find something more than parenting to fill your days. Most women do find something beyond a baby to occupy their time once the hysteria of the first few months has passed. Think about what you really need.

After three weeks at home with my baby, I got frightened. Sometimes I really resented him. My husband and I had never fought until we had the baby. I was so angry that our relationship had changed, and I really resented the baby for it. Then I resented Bill. He still had a job, a world that extended beyond the walls of our apartment. It took me a long time to readjust to my new role in life.

More than anything else in these first three months, the change in your role—from wife to mother, from husband to father—will be the cause of conflict between you and your spouse. Even your differing opinions on childrearing will be less of a critical issue—after all, the baby isn't really old enough yet to be a huge discipline problem. And this conflict isn't simply a matter of who does what for the baby when, but an issue of who your spouse thinks you are now that the baby is home, and who you think you are.

Many couples allow a child to determine their identity and establish a pattern for their interaction. "I'm a mother now. I act uninterested in anything other than my baby. I don't take care of myself. I see my husband as my Daddy and a paycheck. My life is my child. I don't have time for anybody else. I am no longer a sexual being." Or, "I can just turn into a couch potato, now. My wife is with the baby all the time. My wife must be my mother now, so I must act like my father. I am no longer a sexual being."

The danger in retreating from intimacy, in using the child as an excuse to no longer relate to your spouse is that sooner or later one of you is going to say, "Well, if I don't need him or her, if he or she is nothing more than an annoyance, why am I in this relationship? I might as well get a divorce." Not a happy thought, but a definite possibility if you allow yourselves to be so overwhelmed by parenting that you lose track of yourselves as a couple in love. The love you feel for each other is what motivated you to have a child, and it should always be at the center of your relationship. Yes, there are three of you now, but you can never forget that first there were two. And, in fact, after the child is grown and out of the house, there will be just the two of you again.

DON'T GET SLOPPY WITH YOUR LIFE

If you are staying at home during this time, it may hardly seem worth getting dressed or doing much about your appearance, but it is important that you do dress, put on makeup, and feel that you are starting the day. You have to develop a personal schedule, one that includes at least one hour for you to take care of yourself so you can feel human.

Your husband has probably gone back to work by now. He is on a schedule and that can help the both of you to work out a program for taking care of a baby and each other. Your husband's work schedule gives you a good base of time around which to build the rest of your day. Build your schedule around the hours when he will be around to help.

Jane, at first, wanted to spare her husband from getting up in the middle of the night for the 3 A.M. feeding. She soon realized she could not continue to be on 24-hour call. She was too exhausted to handle the baby all day long. After some discussion, she and Herman realized that they could work out a better arrangement. Instead of getting up at 7 A.M., Herman would wake up at 6 A.M. and give the baby a bottle. That meant Jane could sleep until at least nine when the baby was once again demanding attention. She was, therefore, able to get in a full six-hour's sleep.

If you and your spouse feel that your lives are now revolving around this baby, that's because it's true. You do have to remind each other in your moments together that this is only for a few months, and that there will be a relief from this fatigue.

Bill and I were almost angry when one of the couples who we'd met in our birthing classes told us that their little girl was sleeping from midnight to 6 A.M. I was up every two hours with Kevin, and some nights I didn't get any sleep at all. It wasn't much easier in the daytime. I couldn't just hold

Kevin. I had to walk with him. I welcomed visitors; they always wanted to hold him. They'd walk the floor with him and I'd finally get a chance to sit down.

Find ways to get help and assistance. It's perfectly OK to have a parent help out while you're home. Or take turns with a friend. Have her come over with her baby and watch both children while you shower and give yourself a beauty treatment. You can do the same for her when she needs help. Build yourself a support system of family and other new mothers. Start with the women you met in your childbirth classes or a neighbor you've always liked. You can all help to make the load a little easier on yourselves.

When your husband comes home, let him take over some of the baby care. Make this the baby's bathtime—Daddy and baby alone, having fun. Or have your husband give all the children a bath while you cook. If you're up to it, you can make this a time you all share together. Whatever works for you is fine, but don't make the mistake of being the caretaker all day long and continue with that role even after your husband comes home. He isn't more exhausted than you are just because he went out to work. You've been working hard all day, too.

THINGS CAN GET CRAZY

Mary and Ralph both had very respectable jobs. Ralph was a sales representative for a publishing company and spent a lot of time out of the office calling on clients, so it was very difficult to reach him by phone. Mary was a criminal lawyer and had spent most of her adult years dealing with difficult people and problems. She assumed nothing could rattle her, least of all a baby, and expected to be in total control of her first months at home.

One day little Peter started crying and nothing would stop him. Mary called her mother. She wasn't home. She called Ralph. His secretary advised her that Ralph was out of the office and unreachable by phone. Mary left a message for Ralph to call her and went back to the baby. An hour later, there was no phone call from Ralph and the baby was still screaming. Mary knew that she couldn't take much more of this. She called Ralph again. The secretary said that he hadn't called in. Well, Mary lost it and demanded to have Ralph paged. She told the secretary that it was a life-and-death crisis and that Ralph must call her back immediately.

The phone rang. I picked it up and didn't even wait for Ralph to say hello. I screamed into the phone. "Get home right now or I'm going to kill your son" and hung up. By the time Ralph got home the baby was fine. I was crying my eyes out, a real mess. We fought. We made up. We realized that we had a problem.

While Mary's reaction may have been extreme, it is likely that it grew from a deep sense of frustration and help-lessness. Nobody really knows what to do with a hysterical infant. It helps, however, if you feel that you have the support of your spouse. The truth that Mary and Ralph discovered was that Ralph wasn't really available to Mary. He was still living by the old rules: "I go out and earn a living and nobody can bother me at my job, no matter what." What they had to find out, and what eventually sent them to counseling, was why Ralph wasn't making himself avail-able to his wife and child. Like so many first-time fathers, he was uncomfortable with the new role and copying the only other father he had ever known, his own, whether or not he was happy with the interaction he shared with his father.

In addition to seeking professional help, there are some things that you can do to make your husband's adjustment to fatherhood a little easier. First, remember that you love him, remember that he doesn't have the same physical bond that you share with the child, think about his past and how it is likely to influence him, and then help him to feel more comfortable with his child. And, don't expect too much too soon. Start by involving him in determining the baby and family schedule. Let him recognize that he must make an important contribution to the family with more than just a paycheck.

CAREER CHANGE

Ben was a trouble-shooter for a computer company. His territory comprised five states, and he was on the road a lot, often without any notice for days or even a week at a time. After Sue had the baby, the travel troubled him more than it did before. He felt that he was missing an important time of his baby's life and wanted very much to be at home every night with his family.

Ben's travel troubled Sue, too. She worked full-time and really couldn't handle the baby alone. It was also hard to be as flexible as they had been in the past to Ben's sporadic and unplanned travels. When Ben learned that an office job at a slightly lower salary was open with his company, he and Sue decided that the cut in pay was worth the time together and he applied for the job. While making a career change or taking a paycut may not delight you, it may solve some of your lifestyle problems.

Some fathers truly can't or won't change their schedules to become involved in an infant's life. It may be that they just can't deal with infants, or this could be an indication of a bigger problem. You must observe and decide if your husband is just the type of guy who won't really appreciate his child until it can run, talk, and walk, or a totally uninterested parent. You may try to convince him that he will come to regret having missed these early months. You may decide to just let him be the parent he can and will be, but whatever tact you do take, it must be something that you both feel comfortable about. Don't push him into anything. He should spend time with his baby because he wants to, or at least learns to want to. Both father and child, forced to spend time together, may grow to resent each other.

If your husband won't change his schedule, then you have to find other people or ways to get help, and you have to engage in some sort of dialogue about what is behind his behavior.

A WOMAN UNDER THE INFLUENCE OF STRESS

What's the first thing that suffers when you're not getting any sleep and feel like the pressure is on all the time? Your disposition and sense of humor. Don't be surprised if you're not a barrel of laughs these first few months. A cute, teasing comment by your husband may not elicit a tickle or a giggle from you when you haven't been off your feet for twenty-four hours. Suddenly, all the overtime he's putting in—even though he may be getting paid for it—becomes a personal insult, something he's doing to get even with you. The way he chews his cereal or puts his socks in the drawer may seem like the most annoying things in the world.

Yes, you are exhausted, but give the guy a break. It's very unlikely that he's doing any of these things just to annoy you. (If he is, then you have a big problem.) Ask him for help, but don't snap at him and criticize him simply because he doesn't roll his socks the way you do—particularly if he good-naturedly volunteered to do six loads of wash so you could relax. It is unfair to treat someone like this at any time, but particularly unfair now when your husband may be trying very hard to learn a whole new way of life. So, let it go. Give the man you love the space to be exactly who he is. Don't demand that he do things the way you would. He may tell you that since you find his method so unsatisfactory, that you just do it yourself.

SANITY SAVERS

Mary was a trauma nurse and felt she could handle anything. She really expected that she'd have a baby and things would just be fine. Well, she had a little boy, and this little boy was the hungriest little boy in the world. He was breastfeeding every hour. In a conversation with a friend Mary said she felt like an all-night diner. She'd nicknamed the baby "the barnacle" because he was just stuck to her. In order to regain her strength, she finally had to have her mother come over every afternoon for four hours or so. Her mother then bottlefed breast milk to the baby while Mary had a nap. While her mother was still there, Mary would take a shower, cook dinner, and be able to greet her husband like a normal sane human being even though she knew she probably wasn't going to get more than two hours of sleep in a row that night.

CREATING TIME TO BE ALONE

At the same time that you're scheduling baby-sitters

and your mommy and daddy time, you should also be scheduling time for you and your spouse to be together, alone, two adult people in love. Get out your calendars and make a date. Maybe 7:30 P.M. Tuesday or Saturday is the night you go out to dinner and talk. Or maybe after you've returned to a normal sex life, you can schedule a romantic evening for two at a swanky hotel—room service and all. There must certainly be a family member or a baby-sitter that you trust enough to take care of your baby overnight. If anything goes wrong, they can always phone you.

This time is truly critical to your sense of identity, your ability to grow as a couple, and to approach your child as a sane, rested parent. Babies are wonderful, but parents really do need some time off for good behavior. Yes, you may talk about nothing but the baby on the first night you go out alone, but you'll get over it, and on your second or third day find yourselves slipping back into normal adult conversations.

MENTAL HEALTH TIME

Time together is important, and so is time totally alone, to put your feet up, read a book, go out for a beer with your friends, whatever it is that will help you to rejuice your batteries and not feel so trapped by your new circumstances.

A RETURN TO SOCIAL LIFE

Well, it's time to make your reentry into the adult social scene. Many new parents first make the step back into this scene by having friends and family to visit. Still uncertain about leaving their infant with a baby-sitter, they opt for a party at home so they can administer to their child if any problem should arise.

Parties at home are a wonderful idea. But you and your spouse must establish certain rules, and you must both stick by them. First, the baby must be asleep before the guests arrive. Any friend or family member who wants a peek at the baby should be advised to either come before the baby's bedtime or hold off until the baby wakes up on its own. Trotting a whole group of half-drunk adults into the baby's room to take a peek is going to upset the baby, probably wake it up and ruin your evening. Everyone thinks a sleeping baby is adorable. A crying baby is another story altogether. If the baby starts crying, you may find yourself in the bedroom alone for the night, walking a screaming infant while everybody else has a good time.

While a baby at a large, boozy party is a bad idea, there's absolutely nothing wrong with having your baby with you when friends come over for a late afternoon brunch. If your friends like children, and they probably do if they want to see the baby, this gives them an opportunity to hold the baby, and it gives you a little break. Let your friend Alice hold the baby while you drink a glass of wine, a cup of coffee, a diet soda.

GUESS WHO'S COMING TO DINNER?

My father was the proudest grandpa I'd ever seen. He was retired and really was a big help in the beginning. I could call him up at almost any time and he'd run an errand for me. He and my mother only lived a few blocks away, so it wasn't uncommon for him to drop over for an impromptu visit. My mother was a little more distant and always used to scold him not to show up unannounced. I couldn't say no to him, though. I mean, after all, he helped so much. Bill didn't feel quite as gracious about it though. He didn't like walking in from work and finding my father sitting at the kitchen table with the baby and a cup of coffee. He wanted time alone with his family. Finally, I had to talk to my father about scheduling his comings and goings a bit better. It was rough. Either he was going to get mad at me or Bill was. Great, huh.

Learning to say no to people is very important right now. You may not mind your father or mother dropping in, but after you have a baby, it's also very likely that every cousin, aunt, and uncle is going to want to stop for a visit. Set some rules. Have visitors when it's convenient for you. If people turn up unannounced and it's really not a very good time, or you were just on your way out the door, then you must tell them so and continue with your plans. Try to schedule people in groups, particularly problem relatives, so there is some other person there to assume the burden of entertaining. And, you can't cook dinner for everybody, so make it very clear from the beginning that this is or isn't an invitation for dinner.

THE BABY LOOKS JUST LIKE . . .

Every relative that does come around to see the new baby will probably have a theory about who the baby looks like (usually them) and what the baby is likely to be when it grows up. This assessment is probably based on something as clever as watching your baby stare cross-eyed at their tie. If your baby has hair, they'll tell you that's weird. If your baby is bald, they'll tell you that's weird. Everybody has an idea of the perfect baby, but not everybody is going to share your positive feelings about your own child.

So, what can you do when your second cousin tells you that your new son looks like her husband did as a baby, and you hate her husband and she knows it? Just ignore it. Bite your tongue, look at your baby and smile. Why these people are telling you all these negative things is far too complicated to analyze now, and it really isn't worth your trying to figure out. Of course, you don't have to expose the baby to people you don't like. But, sometimes people you deeply love can say some pretty dumb things, too. Try very hard not to let these comments influence you and your husband. Just remember that they are this other person's way of expressing some feelings that has nothing to do with you or your baby. A very nervous grandmother, for example, or a grandmother who doesn't like the idea of being old enough to be a grandmother, may be reading negative connotations into every freckle, burp, and sleepless night.

If the hurtful comments are coming from someone you are close to, talk to the offending party. Let them know that their comments are not helping you right now. Suggest that you talk to them about why the baby seems to be bothering them so much. If they are not willing to meet you halfway, then it's time to spend a lot less time with this person. You do have the right to keep your baby out of the clutches of family members or friends who don't seem to share your good feelings about the baby. Sooner or later they will get the message and return to a positive, loving relationship with you and your infant.

BREASTFEEDING, PART II

While it has been well-documented that breastfeeding does provide both physical and emotional advantages for the mother and the baby, it also brings with it certain difficulties. First of all, the mother is then the only one who can provide food, unless we revive the wet nurse. In addition, it means accepting that you will have to be the only parent on constant call. It also means postponing your return to your normal weight, strength, and appearance.

On the other hand, breastfeeding creates a very special time, a sharing experience that you and your spouse should take advantage of. Many men have a secret desire to see what it's like to nurse. Let him try it. Indulge his fantasy and enjoy the fullness and maternal feeling of your breasts. Skip the late news or whatever else you watch on television and make the experience playful. Let him be the baby. Enjoy yourselves and relax.

Also, don't be afraid to let the baby join you and your husband in bed. This is a good way to catch a few extra minutes of sleep. Have your husband bring the baby into your bed when he leaves for work in the morning. This is not going to discourage the baby from sleeping it its own bed. And, don't be afraid that this will disturb the child's sexual development. Children can benefit from some healthy closeness with their parents. Even as they get older, around five or six, they may have nightmares or be frightened at night. It's perfectly okay for them to crawl into bed with mommy and daddy for a little while. The question of how much is healthy can often be answered by examining two simple issues. Is crawling in with mommy and daddy a delaying tactic the child uses to avoid bedtimes? Are you doing this because the child needs it or satisfying some need of your own? Mothers and fathers can be too close to their children and this can both confuse the child and destroy your marriage.

I'M ONE BIG BREAST

Now that the baby is here and everything is fine, you may feel that it's about time your body was your own again. Unfortunately, as long as you're breastfeeding, it's not. Your breasts are going to tell you what to do. They are going to tell you when the baby wants to eat, no matter what. Your baby and your breasts are so in tune, so synchronized that when it's time to eat, they may start leaking milk before the baby starts to nurse.

> *I had Ben in the carriage and we were tearing through the park. I'd taken him shopping. It was Christmas. I had so much to buy. I really thought I could get everything done and get home in time for his afternoon feeding. Well, two o'clock came and went. My breasts were killing me. He's screaming, and I'm leaking through my bra and sweater, praying the milk doesn't stain the lining of my new coat. Finally, we're about a block from the house, waiting for the light to change. I'm in such a state. This old woman taps me on the shoulder and says, "Lady, your baby is crying." I thought I was going to kill her.*

Many women list among their most embarrassing moments the first night they went out to a restaurant in a pretty blouse, and all of a sudden the milk is coming through. What do you do? Well, there isn't much you can do to hide it. You could leave the restaurant and go home, or you could dress in some way to conceal possible accidents. It's things like this that keep many women out of chic clothes and adult situations until they've stopped breastfeeding.

IT'S ONLY NATURAL

We live in a breast-fixated culture. Just go to any

newsstand, and observe men watching a woman walk in the room. Notice how women size each other up. It's no wonder that everybody gets uptight when they imagine themselves feeding their baby in a roomful of people—even friends.

Somehow, however, breastfeeding transcends the purient breast fixations of most people. It is something, in fact, that people generally love the idea of and love to watch. The entire world seems to approve of a nursing mother, so, do feel comfortable taking your baby around to visit. When it's time to nurse, feel free to get comfortable in a quiet corner of the room, or if you are in a public space, find a comfortable restroom.

IT'S NOT NECESSARILY FOR EVERYBODY

I waited the few days it took for the milk to come in. I was dying to experience this. I held Michele at my breast. She'd suck for a while; then she'd cry. So I'd try again and again. She just wasn't getting enough to eat. I knew it. My breasts would barely feel ready for her feedings. I couldn't possibly be making enough milk. But I wanted to breastfeed really badly. When I finally gave it up, some people had some very hurtful things to say about it.

Some mothers, no matter how large or small their breasts, cannot produce enough milk or healthy milk for their babies. This can happen for any number of reasons, infections, blocked milk ducts, or it can simply be an accident of nature. Some mothers don't want to nurse. If you must return to work very soon after delivery, it will be much easier to avoid leaks if you have never gotten your body into the breastfeeding cycle. Some mothers don't feel comfortable about breastfeeding, are too nervous, and some babies just don't take to it—the breast milk may upset their stomachs, the sucking may be too arduous for them, or they may just need a lot more food than their mother can produce.

If your heart is set on breastfeeding, it may be difficult to accept the defeat, but don't pay any attention to those women who may act like you are starting your child off on an unhealthy path. How you feed your baby is your choice. Your baby will do just as well on a bottle. There's no reason to disrupt your entire life just to breastfeed.

> *I would get so embarrassed every time I pulled out Michele's bottle. There would always be someone who would quip, "Oh, you're not breastfeeding." At first I felt that I had better offer an explanation; after all this must make me an inferior mother. When I saw that Michele didn't seem to be suffering for it, and that we shared as much closeness during our feeding time, I really started to feel differently. Instead of apologizing for myself, I'd just answer whoever asked with a simple yes.*

Julie's experience is a good example of how your ideas or fantasies about you and your infant might not all be realized. Being a good parent means being able to go beyond what you'd hoped for, making the best of what reality offers, and accepting that you are not the only person involved in determining what will or won't happen in your family. Your baby, young and helpless though it may be, has a will and desire all it's own. Even at this early stage, you must begin to learn to respect what your child wants, needs, and can handle as a person. If breastfeeding is not something that your baby is interested in, then it's better abandoned. Your baby should be able to have some impact on the way and what it gets to eat.

> *I wasn't so worried about what Michele would feel. Bob was the one who concerned me. Throughout the pregnancy, he waxed rhapsodical on the earth mother image of me with the baby at my breast. He practically painted a picture of us in a log cabin, him out chopping logs for the fire, while I churned butter and breastfed at the same time. This guy was a banker. I couldn't figure out where all this was coming from. His hippie youth maybe? All I knew, was that it really worried me to tell him that I couldn't breastfeed. I thought he'd be crushed.*

Yes, husbands are romantics, too. They too believe that their child, their family, and their life will be perfect, will make up for everything that they missed growing up. A new baby somehow reminds us all of what we yearn for. If your husband is normally idealizing your breastfeeding future, it may hurt you to break the news to him and disappoint him a little, but he should generally just be able to get on with things. Bottlefeeding the baby will, after all, provide him with many more paternal bonding experiences.

If your husband is really thrown by the fact that breastfeeding is out of the question, seems angry at you because you can't perform what he considered an essential function, than you've got another problem altogether. This is something that will definitely require long hours of discussion between the two of you. Your husband will probably come to realize that his expectation is unrealistic and that how you feed your baby has little or nothing to do with his image of himself and acceptance of you. If talking alone doesn't help, this may be the time to seek marriage or individual counseling. You are dealing with a much bigger issue here than simple breastfeeding.

RIGHT/WRONG

Parents and grandparents especially who come from an old-fashioned, more-regimented and less-accepting school of child rearing often feel that there is a right way and a wrong way to handle a child. That the child must, even at a few months of age, conform to what is the right thing to do when it is time to do it. Everything should be scheduled—feedings, sleep—and there should be no deviation in that schedule.

There truly is no right or wrong way to do anything. The best way to discover what is right is to learn what makes you and your baby happy. John and Mary, for example, both worked until 9:30 P.M. every night. As new parents, they both wanted to spend as much time with their baby as possible. So, as soon as they got home, little David was picked up out of his crib and brought in to play with Mommy and Daddy. At first, their baby-sitter went nuts. She threatened to quit, and when John and Mary told her that was fine, she soon decided that maybe she should adapt David's day-time schedule so that he could share this time with his parents.

Schedules are only important when everybody benefits from them. If you face the choice of deciding between a baby on a rigid schedule or time to shower your child with love and affection, you'd be best to opt for the affection. John, Mary, and David simply turned their day around. Yes, relatives were shocked that David was still up at one o'clock in the morning, but the baby didn't seem to suffer because of this unorthodox schedule.

Now, this isn't going to work in every situation. By not having an established bedtime for your baby, life can become more difficult for the parents. There is no set time for them to be alone and share adult time together or time for each of them to be totally alone. You may not feel this is a big issue in the early days with your infant, but it is essential to your return to normal life. Everyone of us does need some time to escape both mentally and physically from the demands of other people.

Mary and John were willing to sacrifice their independent time. They felt that spending more time with David would make him a much happier and freer child. They did also recognize that sooner or later David would have to conform to a normal schedule. In the early months, however, they felt it was better for David's schedule to conform to their unique lifestyle.

A JOINT DECISION

Whatever schedule you do establish must be agreed upon and meet the needs of both parents. Scheduling is an issue that can become a deep conflict between parents. It is an aspect of child rearing that seems to have two distinct and differing attitudes. There are those who believe a schedule must be set right from the beginning and those who believe scheduling inhibits a child's creative development. If you and your husband embrace opposing points of view, you should first try to decide what is motivating your opinions. You will most likely learn that this is another case in which you are positively or negatively reacting to what did or did not happen in your childhood. Once you have accepted what is motivating you, you can then reach a mutual agreement as to how to create the baby and life that you want, instead of reacting to your past.

> *Dom thought it was real cute to rush home and wake up*
> *Chris. Chris would scream. At 6:30 at night he was ready*
> *for a few hours of sleep. But Dom still woke him up. The*
> *baby would scream on and off for about an hour. The next*
> *day would be real torture. Dom really started annoying me.*
> *One night I raced him down the hall and practically threw*
> *my body in the doorway so he couldn't get to the crib. We*
> *talked. It turns out Dom's father wasn't around for the first*
> *few months of his life. He felt all his life that something was*
> *really missing from his childhood. As an adult, his mother*
> *had finally revealed to him that she and his father had been*
> *separated when he was born. Dom was desperate to make*
> *sure that Chris knew that he was there.*

Terry and Dom finally reached a decision that worked
for both of them. Chris would always wake up by himself at
8:00 P.M., so they could have dinner as soon as Dom got
home, clean up right away, and that would leave plenty of
time to spend with Chris. Everybody won with this new
plan. Chris got the sleep he needed, Dom got time with his
son, and Terry had a normal day.

MAKE ROOM FOR DADDY

Barry and Gwen had their first baby after they'd been
married only two years. They were both delighted to have a
little boy. For Barry, it was a dream come true. Gwen had
never gone to work, so many of the conflicts other couples
face did not trouble them. She was quite comfortable assuming the role of housekeeper and mother, and since she
was dedicated to being home with her baby all day, she felt

absolutely no need to plan a schedule. Little James was going to run her life. Whatever the baby wanted at whatever time, she was there to provide. She ate with the baby on her lap, watched television or read with the baby in her arms. If it was a choice between a dinner with the baby on her lap or dinner alone with Barry, the baby always won.

Barry loved James. He loved to spend time with him when he got home in the evening. But, he also loved his wife and wanted the baby to be in bed at a certain time so that he could spend time alone with her. He had a very high-pressure job that sometimes left him feeling insecure. The time he spent with Gwen helped him to regain some perspective and was something he was unhappy to give up.

Gwen, however, could not part with James. If he cried at night, she was up in a flash and immediately brought him back to their bed. Barry felt that verbalizing his anger over Gwen's disappearance into motherhood would only present him as a hateful father. He didn't want Gwen or James to feel that he wasn't happy in his new role. However, he was growing to resent his son. After begging for Gwen's affection and then fighting for it, Barry soon forfeited to his infant and transferred his passion for his wife to an obsession with his job. At least there, he felt, people listened to him and liked him.

Barry's day now ran to at least nine P.M. every night. He was so tired when he got home that it didn't bother him to see his wife and son curled up in front of the television. Barry wasn't the type to have an affair. Instead he developed an alcohol problem. Gwen was then forced to face what was happening to her marriage.

Barry and Gwen's problems may seem extreme; however, they are not terribly rare. They are a good example of what happens when one member of the couple is abandoned in a marriage, or when two people don't have a mutual understanding of how they are going to deal with the change in their lives.

Circumstances out of their control and a lack of communication created a whole different set of problems for Dorothy and Ralph. Ralph lost his job right after the baby arrived, so it was decided that he'd be the one to stay home for the first three months. He could take care of the baby and search for a new job. While this did work out for awhile, Ralph became so attached to the infant, so involved that he decided on his own that he was not going to return to work. When he announced to Dorothy that he felt it was better for the baby for him to stay home, she almost fainted. There was no discussion. Dorothy felt convinced that Ralph would come to his senses sooner or later.

A year went by and Ralph made no effort to find a job. Dorothy was furious. She had never agreed to be the sole supporter of their family. Ralph had broken their original agreement. He had taken what was meant to be a stop-gap measure and turned it into a permanent situation. The big question for Dorothy was: Who was he really doing this for, himself or the baby, and what did it say about his feelings for her?

NO GOOD FOR ANYBODY

This behavior is not going to help anyone. It's destructive to the couple and to the child. One parent soon grows to resent or distance themselves from the child, and the child really does become far more self-centered and spoiled than anyone outside of the family will ever tolerate.

No child, no matter how much they are loved should ever be treated as though they are more important than any other member of the family. In other words, a husband or wife should not treat their spouse as someone who is now less important to them because there is a baby. A relationship with any one member of a family should focus on what is good for that person in the context of the entire family.

Sometimes the needs of the child do come first, particularly in the case of an infant who is totally helpless. Yes, you will have to walk the floors, thereby ignoring your need for a full-night's sleep, but there is no reason to sacrifice your marriage in the name of doing the best for your child.

So, it is for the health of the child, as much as for the couple, that you must be attentive to each other. The parents who have forgotten they are married can be made aware of their behavior before it reaches the point of no return. If friends or family are telling you that you're ignoring or mistreating each other, don't tell them to mind their own business. Think about what they're saying, particularly if you are hearing this from more than one person. Also, if you and your spouse seem to be having the same fight over and over again, it's time to take a serious look at what's going on.

WHAT'S BEHIND IT ALL?

There is a popular myth that husbands cheat in the first months of their baby's life because their wives can't have sex. Well, maybe this isn't the case at all. Maybe they cheat on their wives because their wives abandon them for their child. We all have abandonment anxieties left from childhood. You must both work very hard to ensure that no one gets left by the wayside because there is a new child.

You must also be painfully honest with yourself and each other. If you are turning your back on your partner, fooling yourself with the old it's-for-the-sake-of-my-child routine, you must examine what is going on. You aren't doing this for the child at all. You are just using your child to avoid intimacy with your spouse—not just sexual intimacy but emotional intimacy as well. Having the child has exacerbated a preexisting problem, and it's time to deal with it.

A RETURN TO SEX

It will take seven weeks to two months before you and your spouse can have satisfactory intercourse again. Hopefully, you have continued with kissing, touching, holding, and other displays of affection. It will help to make the readjustment back to a normal sex life much easier.

Post-pregnancy sex is at best awkward and at worst painful. If you are nursing, your hormone balance is high on the progesterone side. This will keep your vagina drier than usual and may make sex painful. Artificial lubricants are a perfect solution to this problem, although they may not be enough for the first time out.

The other problem a lot of couples suffer when considering a return to sex results from the realization that sex may result in pregnancy, which leads to labor and a big responsibilities. While you may love your baby very much, you certainly don't want to go through what you've just gone through in only another nine months.

And don't believe that because you've just had a baby you can't get pregnant. It's very easy to get pregnant again right after delivering your first child. Many couples feel that because they've done without sex for so long they want this first time to be spontaneous and wonderful. They don't want birth control to get in the way, and they end up with another pregnancy. We all know people who have kids who are less than a year apart. Well, this is probably how it happened.

Couples who did not plan the first child and really don't want another but can't face an abortion may find the return to sex extremely difficult. A major reason many men have difficulty is that after the birth of their child, they transfer their feelings about their own mother or mothers in general to their wife. Thinking about her as a sexual being, therefore, becomes almost impossible.

Margaret came into therapy complaining that her husband was paying more attention to the baby than to her. "I feel like I'm nothing, like I'm not important anymore," she confided. "Steve never loved me that much." However, with a little prodding, a more serious problem came to light. Her husband had become almost totally impotent after she gave birth.

By and large, almost all prospective parents have an innate awareness that when a baby comes along, they will have to share their spouse's love and affection. This presents no major problem for those who are fairly secure within themselves; yet for those who aren't, they may find themselves acting less like a parent and more like a jealous sibling.

However, in Margaret's case, the issue wasn't merely insecurity on her part. There was a marked and dramatic difference in her husband's sexual behavior—and that provided the key.

Although Steve feigned fatigue, he had unconsciously transferred strong maternal feelings to his wife and now she was more of a mother in his eyes than a sexual partner. Small wonder he was focusing all of his energy on the child. It was less frightening than examining the source of his impotence.

Feelings of transference occur to some extent in all husband/wife relationships, particularly after the birth of a child. It's normal, so normal that years ago men commonly referred to their wives as "mother. " The difficulty arises only when the transference becomes the dominant force controlling the actions of one or both partners.

This is a time when your identity and sexual identity can be as confusing as it was when you were an adolescent. And just like adolescence you will either adapt to this change easily, become fixated on it, or fight it tooth and nail. Suddenly the deep commitment that marriage and adulthood brings with it is reality. You may have wanted a spouse, a baby, and all the pressures and anxieties they bring with them, but when you actually achieve your goal the prospects can be a bit daunting. You are now responsible, now committed and now very confused.

IS THE BABY OKAY?

If you are first-time parents, you may have read a ton of baby-care and development books, but you're still not really sure what your baby is supposed to be doing at what week in its life. If you have other children, you may notice that your second child isn't developing at the same rate or in the same way as your first.

He sleeps more than the first baby or sleeps less. Eats more or less. Cries or doesn't cry. Moves around or doesn't move. Anything the baby does or doesn't do that you have decided is normal can send you into a real panic. The best thing to do is to ask your doctor at the baby's weekly checkup. Then try to remember that every baby is different and you can't really compare your baby's actions with any of your other children or your friend's children.

THE SPONGE STAGE

You've heard lots of people say it and for a good

reason. Don't fight in front of the baby, yes, even a day old baby. There's a common misconception that infants aren't really taking in what's going on around them, that they're just blank walls because they don't yet understand language. Well, a child may not understand the meaning of your words, but they are very in tune to inflection and attitude. Shouting, a nervous voice, a trembling hand, an uncomfortable, angry, or upset parent can deeply disturb an infant. All these emotions, all these signals of distress and anxiety are communicated through simple body contact or the sounds the baby hears during your conversation. If infants sense that the person holding them is not safe, they will cry. If they sense you are deeply frustrated with them because they're sick, they cry.

Some popular psychologists believe, in fact, that a person's entire life in shaped in these very early months of their life. As infants and children we do not have the screening mechanisms that we develop as adults. We do not have the resources to take something in, assess it, understand it, and not personalize it. Infants are emotionally defenseless. A child who is constantly overhearing her parents fight, her mother worry, or her father drink too much will definitely develop a sense that home is not a secure place, that her parents don't like each other, and that therefore her position in the house is uncertain.

Joan's mother, for example, was extremely nervous. Joan was a second child, born when her mother, Ann, and father, Harry, were living through a rough patch in their marriage. Ann was a nervous wreck for Joan's entire first two years of life. The baby was surrounded by anxiety. When her father was around, there were fights. When he wasn't, his mother cried and walked the floor.

Eventually, Joan and Harry worked out their differences. Harry returned home. Joan, a very sensitive child, watched her parents from the sidelines, tentative, anxious to do everything right so there would be no more fighting. At three she developed stomach problems. When she started kindergarten, her teacher was concerned she had a learning disability. Joan simply couldn't perform when asked to do anything. She'd just fall apart. Joan was tested and found to be extremely intelligent, in fact, gifted, but the teachers were never really able to get much out of her.

While we can't say that bad performance in school is always attributable to a problem at home, it is generally the case. In Joan's case, she was absorbing so much stress at home, was so overstressed and frightened that every action she took would create another problem for her parents that she just collapsed when asked to do the most normal things. She just couldn't handle it. Her little mind was working overtime already.

Now, this isn't to say that you should create a fantasyland around your child either. Teaching a child that there is no conflict in life is just as unhealthy as teaching them that everything is a trauma. Balance is key and abuse wears many disguises. Children who grow up believing that every action they take is wrong, who learn failure young, and who are surrounded by anger and frustration may live under the same spectre as children who were physically abused. The environment that you create for your child should be one in which every personality is allowed to develop freely, in which everyone is accepted and loved for who they are and what they're individually capable of.

SPARE THE ROD

Our society is just now breaking away from some pretty twisted theories of child rearing. For hundreds of years, religious fanatics and supposed authorities have spread some pretty ugly ideas about the role of children. (They should be seen and not heard, hit when they step out of line, do only their parent's bidding.) Infants and children are not willful monsters desperate to be tamed into responsible adults. They're people with developing personalities and a capacity for life that should be as positively influenced as possible. We can all learn something from our children. After all, one of the beautiful things about having children is to re-create something that life has taken away from us adults.

SUMMING UP

You've done it. You've brought a brand new person into the world and have taken the first steps toward establishing a relationship with this utterly unique, constantly growing individual.

Babies have no monopoly on development and change, of course. As time passes, you, your partner, and your child will find again and again that your life together is not a destination or even a series of events, but a process by which you all grow simultaneously, adjust to the new circumstances, and grow again. May you share the deep satisfaction and fulfillment that accompanies freely sharing and rejoicing in this growth with the others with whom you have decided to share your life.

INDEX

life choices, previous 57-58
listening, importance of, 35, 78-79, 98-99
living quarters, 123-124

medical help in conception, 53-56, 60-61
medical choices in pregnancy, 78, 120-122, 145-158
miscarriage, 104-105
mistakes, 177
morning sickness, 81-84
motivations of parents in having a baby, 19-21
myths about childbirth, 162-163

nesting instinct, 138-139

parents' reaction to pregnancy, 76-78
performance anxiety in lovemaking, 46-48
physical appearance and weight, 167
physical symptoms of pregnancy, 71-72
postpartum depression, 185-187
pregnancy tests, 63-65
premature delivery, 143-144
preparation for delivery, 145-147
pressure, defusing, 27, 50, 51-52
problems in labor, 150-152

quiet time, importance of, 103

reactions to birth, 149-150